Our
Presbyterian
Belief

Our Presbyterian Belief

FELIX B. GEAR

John Knox Press
ATLANTA

Library of Congress Cataloging in Publication Data
Gear, Felix B.
    Our Presbyterian belief.

    Includes bibliographical references.
    1. Theology, Presbyterian.   I. Title.
BX9175.2.G43   230′.5′1   79–23421
ISBN 0–8042–0676–7

Copyright © 1980 John Knox Press, Atlanta
Printed in the United States of America

Contents

1.

Our Presbyterian Belief About GOD

Our Presbyterian belief begins with God. Our faith has often been called a God-centered religion, and this is in reality a very good description of it. There is no better place for us to begin our study of the teachings of our Church than with the thought of God—he is the starting point of the Presbyterian system of belief; he is all in all. There is a sense in which we could say that the Bible is primarily concerned with God and his relation to humanity, which is simply another way of saying that we not only derive our existence from God but also our value and the meaning of life.

Before we begin to think about God and his relation to us and to the world, it may be helpful to say a few words about the study of Christian beliefs. It is often thought that doctrine is a dull, dry, drab subject and that it is too deep for the average Christian. Nothing could be farther from the truth. We may well ask, as a modern British theologian, Dorothy Sayers does, what could be more exciting, more thrilling, more dramatic, more stirring, more moving than the story of how the eternal God, the Creator of all things, came down to earth and took upon himself human form, living in our midst and finally dying for us? Nor is the study of Christian doctrine as difficult or complicated as is sometimes thought.

It may be somewhat surprising to learn that we can actually sum up everything that has been thought, said, or written in this field in about *ten words*, small ones at that, *none of which is more than one syllable.* We can list them as follows:

1. God, 2. Man, 3. Sin, 4. Grace, 5. Truth, 6. Christ, 7. Church, 8. Signs, 9. Life, 10. End.

(*Note*: The word "man" is used to designate both men and women, and has been retained at times in accordance with the author's design as stated above.)

For the most part we shall follow this simple scheme throughout our entire study, although there will be minor modifications from time to time so as to make our study as clear as we can. We shall now begin to think about God.

1. What Difference Does the Belief in God Make in Our Life?

(1) The View of a Psychologist

First, let us ask ourselves the question, "What difference does it make whether or not a person believes in God?" The Psalmist had been thinking of this question when he exclaimed, "The fool has said in his heart there is no God" (Psalm 14:1). Many people, especially in modern times, have tried to discard the idea of God as a worn-out superstition. The philosopher Nietzsche said, "God is dead," and the way in which he put it we believe he must have added "Thank God." Two of our greatest psychologists have grappled with this subject and have enabled us to realize that, after all, man cannot get on very well in life without God. William James held that if ever we come to the conclusion that there is no God, our energies will dry up and our wills become paralyzed. We will lose all hope and will ultimately sink into utter despair. It is his opinion that we cannot stand the thought of living in a world without God and that a belief in God will become an almost unlimited source of energy. He is saying very much the same thing as the Psalmist tells us in the words, "But the way of the ungodly shall perish" (Psalm 1:6).

(2) What a Great Russian Thinker Says

The great Russian novelist and psychologist, Dostoevsky, held to a view similar to that of James but expressed it differently. He did not believe that man's energies would ever dry up nor his will become inert, but that once the thought of God drops out of a man's consciousness he will spend his time, abilities and energies in trying to exert his own will and express his own ego. He will become a law unto himself and will seek only his own desires and end in life. He will have no regard for others and he will not be governed by any moral principles. But he can never be as big or as bad a cosmic rebel as he wants to be, and he will ultimately become frustrated and end up in hopeless self-destruction. That man needs God has always been the conviction of our Presbyterian belief as expressed in *The Shorter Catechism:* "Man's chief end is to glorify God, and to enjoy him forever."

2. Is There a God?

One of our leading European religious thinkers has said that anyone who asks the question, "Is there a God?" is mad. The writers of both the Old and New Testaments took God as much for granted as they did the world, other people, or the air they breathed. They believed that everything that is, is in God; that there is nothing that is not in God. The truth is we can know nothing at all in life without knowing it in God, for all things exist in him. Augustine was right when he said that he could not even know himself without knowing that both the world around him and he himself were dependent upon some other power or being. If, therefore, it is true that a person cannot know himself without knowing God, for him to ask the question, "Is there a God?" is as absurd as to ask himself, "Is there a me?" In short, for one to realize that he is a person is also to feel that he is a creature whose life has been given him by some power not his own. It was with this same thought that John Calvin, the founder of the Presbyterian Church, opened his great work on Christian doctrine. He said that all our human wisdom may be summed up in knowledge of God and knowledge of self.

3. How Does God Make Himself Known?

(1) God Is Known in Three Persons

When we come to consider the Scriptures we will think about God's revelation of himself from a different point of view than that we are now discussing. Here we are simply asking the question that when God does make himself known in revelation, how does he do it? It is our conviction that God reveals himself to man in three persons; as Father, Son, and Holy Spirit. This is what we speak of as the doctrine of the Trinity. The writers of the New Testament came to believe that God does manifest himself in this three-fold way because of their own experiences in fellowship with him. They also believed firmly that in spite of the different ways in which God manifested himself to them there is only one God.

(2) God as Father

They knew God to be the ground or source of all that there is, especially the giver of life to them. It is out of this experience of complete dependence upon God that our Presbyterian belief has come which stresses what we call the "Sovereignty of God." We believe that just as we are absolutely dependent upon God for physical life we are also dependent upon him for our spiritual life and all its blessings. We may illustrate this sense of dependence which all of the biblical writers seemed to have felt from Milton's *Paradise Lost*. Eve is shown standing in the Garden of Eden fully realizing for the first time that she is. She looks all around her in the garden, at herself, her body, her hands and her feet; she surveys her powers of sight and movement in utter amazement. She exclaims, "What am I?" "What am I doing here?" It is this sense of dependence on another that the writers of the Bible give us so clearly.

(3) God as Son

The New Testament writers also had a strange new experience in their companionship with Christ. They knew Christ as one who loved them ultimately as God only could love them. They knew his forgiving power, and that God only could forgive sins. They also knew his ability to change their lives. They came finally to realize that these things which they were finding in Christ were the very things which God alone could give them or do for them. They also came to see that the quality of life which Christ brought to them was stronger than death. In the resurrection of Christ they saw him as conqueror of death, hell, and the grave. They knew as all men know that if there is any power which can overcome death, it is divine power. Christ not only claimed to have the power to forgive sins and conquer death, he exercised this power. Thus they knew in their own experience who he was—nothing less than God himself.

(4) God as the Holy Spirit

To understand their experience of the Holy Spirit, which led them to the conviction that he is a divine power, we must go to Pentecost. We are told that there were one hundred and twenty persons in the Upper Room. They were Jews from practically every then known country. We may be sure, therefore, that there had been brought together all the human passions, hatreds, prejudices, fears, and sins that could be found in any similar cross-section of humanity then and now. A British professor once said to his university class something like this: There are enough hatreds, jealousies, prejudices, and fears in this room to start a major war. This was equally true of those who had come together at Pentecost.

All at once something very new and strange occurred. This motley group began to have a sense of "togetherness" never known before. They felt that they belonged together, that they had all things in common, and that there their purposes in life were the same. In a word, these people who had been isolated from each other by their human passions suddenly realized that they loved one another. The power of love was at last loose in their hearts. Their interpretation of this tremendous change of attitude toward each other—even to the extent of being willing to share their possessions—was that God was in their midst as a personal power changing them. This wonderful power they knew to be the Holy Spirit. Our Christian faith has always thought of the Holy Spirit as being identical with love in God, and as being the power that makes for wholeness in human lives.

(5) What the Creeds Say

As the New Testament writers recorded these experiences which have been mentioned above, and in the light of their interpretation of them we have the basic materials and facts that have gone into the statement of the Christian doctrine of the Trinity. All Christian thinkers know that it is not possible to explain the doctrine of the Trinity; nor is it possible accurately to illustrate it. The creeds of the Church have simply tried to say that God is one and yet he manifests himself to man as three persons; Father, Son, and Holy Spirit. While each manifestation is of the same God none of the three ways in which God discloses himself is exactly the same—each is distinctive.

4. How Can We Speak of God?

(1) Non-Christian Notions

People have always been concerned with the question, "What can we say about God?" There have been those who have wanted to be able to say anything about God regardless as to whether or not it was consistent. We usually find this tendency in pantheism—the view that everything is God. The great philosopher Spinoza belonged to this type of thinker. Again, there are those who have held that God is too great, too big, really too far above man for us even to say anything about him. Our Christian faith, however, holds to a position between these two extremes. We believe that we can say some things about God but that we cannot say everything.

(2) The Christian Conception

Perhaps the best expression of this view is to be found in *The Shorter Catechism:* "God is a Spirit, infinite, eternal, and unchangeable, in his being, wisdom, power, holiness, justice, goodness, and truth." Let us look at what the Catechism has to say about God. In speaking of God as Spirit we learn that we cannot identify him with the physical world. It means that essentially he is a personal being and capable of entering into relationships with the persons he has created. To say that God is infinite and eternal means that you cannot limit God as to his person, knowledge, or power. God has always been and always will be: His existence does not depend upon anything outside himself. We believe God knows all things all the time. God can do everything according to his Holy will; that is, he has the power to achieve his own loving purpose. He is not limited by time and space as we are. Some one has said that his center is everywhere, his circumference nowhere. God always acts in perfect wisdom; he is holy which we can take to mean that he is above us as a divine being, but also that God is above all evil. To say that he is a God of justice means not only that he will deal with his creatures in all fairness and equity but also that he expects men so to deal, with each other, and above all, to give him what he is due. We believe that he is good, as the giver of life, the bounties of nature, and of his redemptive love in Christ. The Catechism does not mention love as a characteristic of God because if he is good we know he is loving. These are some of the things we can say about God.

5. What Does God Do?

(1) God Creates

The Bible tells us that God does three things: He creates, he controls, he redeems. God created everything thing that exists out of nothing. This is our Christian conviction. We do not know what it means to make something out of nothing, since it is quite beyond our human experience. A housewife cannot make a cake out of nothing, a mechanic cannot make a car out of nothing, even an author cannot make a book out of nothing. Neither can an artist paint a picture out of nothing. But the writing of a book or the painting of a picture are more like what we think of when we say that something is made out of nothing. We cannot point to anything out of which God made the world. This is, he did not make it from anything outside himself; nor did he make it from any part of himself. It is solely the result of his creative will or word.

The glorious part about God's creative power is that he continues to exercise it in the continuous support and control of the world. God is still creating according to some of our leading scientists. At this very moment he is bringing new worlds into existence. He is creating on such a vast scale that our minds get dizzy to think of it. We are informed by some scientists that there is coming into our universe from the outside, gaseous substances that congeal and harden into stars and planets. Every second the amount of this material is as large or larger than our globe. It is computed as a nillion tons—100,000,000,000,-000,000,000,000,000,000,000.

(2) God Governs

God's control of the world is what we call *providence* although this is also a continuation of his creative power. We believe that God exercises his providential care over the world in general, over individuals like ourselves, and especially over the Church. Ways in which God's providence is carried out may be seen in the different levels of creation; he deals with inanimate things, plant and animal life, and human persons in varying ways to achieve his purpose in the world. Also, he works through the laws of nature, the moral principles of human nature, and through the personal lives of men and women to achieve his goals. Even nations are used for God for the working out of his will in the world. One of the chief ways in which God's providence is manifest is through prayer. He often works through miracles, too.

(3) God Redeems

We come now to God's work of redemption. I think we can say reverently that this is the biggest and hardest work God has to do—the changing of human lives like yours and mine. We see God at work in the Old Testament to deliver Israel over and over again. Israel is chosen as a divine instrument of redemption. Her great figures like Abraham and Moses are selected by God for redemptive purposes. It is clear from the Old Testament that in both creation and in the history of Israel it is God's intention to make redemption world-wide. We find the same truths set forth in the New Testament. Some New Testament scholars believe God's purpose in creation was to establish the Church on earth, as his redeemed people so he could say what was spoken through the prophet Isaiah, "That I may plant the heavens, and lay the foundations of the earth, and say unto Zion, Thou art my people."

We can recognize God at work, therefore, in all three of these ways—as Creator, Ruler, and Redeemer. These are the things he is doing all the time; to such activities as these Jesus referred when he said, "My Father worketh even until now, and I work" (John 5:17). Christian thought has ascribed creation, including the control of the world, to God as father. The work of redemption when we think of it from the beginning of faith until the fulfillment in glory is attributed to Christ the Son and to the Holy Spirit. The atoning work of Christ begins our salvation and the Holy Spirit completes it.

Suggested Reading:

A Call to Faith, Rachel Henderlite (John Knox Press, 1955).

Introduction to the Reformed Tradition, John H. Leith (John Knox Press, 1977).

Presbyterians, Their History and Beliefs, Walter L. Lingle and John W. Kuykendall (John Knox Press, 1978). Helpful for the background of Presbyterianism.

Confession of Faith, Chapters, 2,3,4, and 5.

Shorter Catechism, Questions 1, 4–12.

Scripture, Genesis 1, 2; Psalms 23, 145; Luke 15.

2.

Our Presbyterian Belief About MAN

What is man? Since the Psalmist asked this question a long time ago, and no doubt before, man has been a subject of controversy. Perhaps there is no area of Christian thought in which there have been greater differences of opinion. Often the great religious movements in the Christian faith have come about as the result of the differing views concerning our nature. This has also been true of many secular tendencies. We see this rather clearly illustrated at the time of the Protestant Reformation in the sixteenth century. It could be said that the reformers pulled away from the Roman Catholic Church because their view of human nature was such that they did not believe man had anything to do with his salvation. Since the time of the Reformation there have been many controversies within Protestantism and many, if not most of them, have centered around this. Again, in the twentieth century we find that theological discussion has been dealing with the same subject and we are coming out with some of the same answers that were set forth in the Christian faith many centuries ago.

1. Why Study Man?

From what we have said already it is no doubt obvious that it is necessary for us to know something about man if we are to be clear in our thinking of the Christian faith. Until we can agree as to what kind of being man is we will have to leave many questions unanswered concerning the faith of the Church, as well as the nature and meaning of life. There are those who believe that man has the ability to live the moral life and therefore has no need of divine grace. Others hold that while man must have the help of divine grace to rise above his fallen human nature, he still has the freedom to choose or reject any offer of salvation that may come to him from his Creator. Still others are convinced that sin so badly affects human nature, and that man is so hopelessly caught in the predicament of sinfulness that he cannot savingly know God nor lift himself out of his sin by his own powers. This is our Presbyterian belief.

While these questions may seem futile or trite to us, they have always been regarded as important issues in the history of Christian thought. For instance, it is possible to show that many of our western institutions, religious, social, political, and educational are the outgrowth of certain convictions about man. Our Presbyterian forefathers believed that we could under God govern ourselves wisely but that because of certain essential traits of our human nature it was necessary to have a system of checks and balances so as to avoid the temptations that come with power and privilege. They believed that human nature is sufficiently self-centered to want to get along without divine help so far as redemption was concerned—we have always found it hard to believe that we could not save ourselves.

Dr. Arnold Toynbee has stated emphatically that the greatest need of our century is not more scientific knowledge but a better understanding of human nature and of human relationships. It is almost ironical that our age which has so effectively conquered outer space is so ineffective in dealing with our "inner space." Critics of our modern western culture and of many of the liberal tendencies in it have pointed out that one of our chief mistakes is our failure to take into account, in a realistic fashion, the nature of man. Christian thought at its best has always tried to view human nature in such a way as to give full expression to the powers of man without ascribing to him those qualities that belong only to God.

2. Where Does Our Concern Lie?

From the Christian point of view our primary interest in man has to do with the relation to God. Of course we want to get all the light that modern philosophy and psychology can throw upon human nature. We are grateful that modern insights into the nature of man enable us to understand man, so we believe, better than our forefathers in the faith. We believe, for instance, that human nature is more dynamic, more fluid, more malleable than was thought by previous generations. We have discovered recently the almost unlimited possibilities that may be in store for us in the realm of our knowledge of humanity, as well as that of nature. But while all of this new knowledge has its place and will be of great assistance in the formulation of the Christian faith for future generations, we can never get away from the fact that our Christian faith is basically concerned with man in his relationship and attitude toward God.

Because our concern with man is essentially religious we are immediately confronted with a universal problem in human nature—the "grandeur and misery" of man. Man can be great and he can be small; both at the same time. He can be generous and selfish. We wonder at his grandeur and we worry about his meanness. This schism in the very nature of man is also vividly described by the Apostle Paul when he said, "I do not understand my own actions. For I do not do what I want, but I do the very thing I hate" (Romans 7:15). It is this contradiction at the core of human personality that makes man an insoluble mystery, a baffling perplexity, and an enigmatic being. He is grounded in nature but also touches the heavens. He has been called a "clod and a wing." He can turn his thoughts inward on himself alone or he can rise above himself—he can make himself miserable or great.

3. What Do Non-Christians Say About Man?

(1) The Scientific View

There are several secular views of man. The current scientific view describes humans in terms of a physical being almost exclusively. Here we are thought of primarily in terms of our relationship to our environment, and of our physical needs. Often our moral failures are ascribed to the hang-over of our instinctive urges. Insofar as man is regarded as being physical this view does not disprove the Christian doctrine, nor is Christian thought necessarily concerned with it.

(2) The Humanitarian Concept

We have also what is frequently called the humanitarian concept of man. This view regards man as capable of almost unequalled power to achieve his own ends and as a self-sufficient being who does not need to depend on any outside help such as a divine being would offer. The trouble with this idea is that it is simply not true to human experience. The last few decades have taught us that we are not self-sufficient. To both of the above views concerning human nature we can say in the words of Jesus, "Man shall not live by bread alone" (Matthew 4:4).

(3) The Rational Theory

There is still a third view which thinks of us as essentially rational creatures. This theory tends to equate sin with ignorance. Its hope of overcoming our human difficulties, frailties, and faults lies in increasing our knowledge and in developing our understanding. This is an old and honored tradition in our western culture and dates from the Renaissance Movement. It was characteristic of the thought of the eighteenth century in both Europe and America.

(4) The Communist Notion

A fourth view has come into prominence in recent years. It is the Marxist or Communistic notion of humanity. Man is placed at the center of the social order. He is a product of nature but nature is also a product of man. Human life is an outgrowth of the economic and social order in which we live but we in turn can, must, and will change that order. Man as such is not evil. Sin, if we may use this term here, roots in man's social and economic systems, especially capitalism. Our chief objection to this view is that it teaches that we live in only one dimension, on only one plane—this world of space and time. We are not related to anything beyond this world. Further, we have nothing but an earthly destiny, while from our Christian point of view man will live again and this life on earth derives its chief inspiration and meaning from the life to come. Communism also buries the individual man in the social order of the community. His economic life and even his inner life are both absorbed into that of the community. In no case is sin due to the evil heart or will of man but is derived from the social milieu. All of the views we have discussed thus far have one thing in common—they do not recognize the "dark streak" in human nature which the Bible calls sin.

4. What Is the Christian View of Man?

(1) Man Is Related to God

We have tried to emphasize the fact that we are basically concerned with man from the religious point of view. Our Presbyterian belief has never dealt with man merely as we find him in his present existence. It has tried to see man as God made him, and God's intention for him in creation. It has also viewed him as he un-made himself by sin and thwarted the divine intention for him. Finally, it has regarded him as God re-makes him in redemption and thus restores to him the destiny which he intended for him in creation. To put it briefly, man is related to God as his Creator, Judge, and Redeemer.

(2) Man Is Created by God

As Creator, God has made man a finite creature. This means that man cannot go it in life all alone; he is tied at the very center of his being to a power beyond himself. Also, God made man in his own image. Thus he is both responsible and free. God could say to us, "I have set the limits of your existence; they are not in your hands but in mine. You are as I made you and your being must follow certain laws. Your happiness and destiny are best found within the scope of my will for you. I expect you to keep my laws. They not only express your highest nature but they also express mine." But man also has freedom. He can rise above himself as no other creature is able to do. He has the ability to distinguish between right and wrong, and as Calvin says, he never loses this power. When he has two choices, one higher and the other lower, and he chooses the lower path his conscience tells him he has done wrong. By being made in the image of God one also was endowed with the capacity to have fellowship with God and with all his fellow creatures who likewise were formed in God's image. Traditionally, we have said that man prior to his fall had inner integrity, ability to do the will of God, proper knowledge of God, and a wise control over the world (Psalm 8).

Our Presbyterian belief has attached much importance to the view that a person is created in the image of God. It means that he can never lose the sense of responsibility that God placed upon him in creation. He can never fully satisfy the cravings of his deeper nature until he returns to God, for God made him for himself and man is overcome with an inner "divine discontent" until he finds God. Further, man can never entirely lose this image of God although as we shall see he can greatly distort it. Consequently, all men have retained a remnant of the image of God and every human being we meet, regardless of character, position, race, color, or creed is to be treated as one who has in him the divine image.

(3) Man Is Judged by God

One is related to God as his Judge because he is a sinner. It is second nature for man, so it seems, to go against God's will. He has an innate tendency to place himself at the center of his own existence where God only rightly belongs. His self-centeredness drives him away from God in pride, rebellion, arrogance, unbelief, and hostility. He realizes that the shadow of God's hand is thrown across the path which he wishes to pursue in the fulfillment of his egoistic wishes. It is as if a traffic signal or a policeman would say to one of us driving the wrong way down the street, "You can't go this way." For an instant we are angry, frustrated, and perhaps bitter. This is the way it is with man when his will clashes with the divine will. He is thrown into a perpetual state of contradiction within himself, in relation to his world, his neighbor, and his God. Everything he undertakes seems to fall short of his wishes, hopes and dreams. He is inclined to use the marvelous gifts God has bestowed upon him—his mind, his affection, his will, the bounties of nature, and his neighbors in an effort to express his own ego and to achieve his own shortsighted aims in life.

He loses that inner integrity which Christian thinkers call holiness, and his inner life becomes shattered to bits and he is torn in many different ways. He can no longer do the things that are pleasing to God because he simply does not want to. He knows there is a God, as we have seen, but he cannot know what kind of God there is. He still has the ability to control the forces of nature but lacks the moral insight to use them wisely. Consequently, he becomes enslaved by the forces of nature. In our time we have seen man make tremendous strides in scientific knowledge. Yet it is generally recognized that he is at a loss to know how to use the marvelous gifts and powers at his disposal. Instead of using his knowledge and skill for constructive purposes he employs his time and abilities thinking up new ways of destroying human life. This has happened until some think "the mind of man has reached the end of its tether."

The arresting fact for Christian faith is that one cannot cure himself of this contradiction into which he has fallen or lift himself out of the predicament into which his folly has plunged him. He may try to get himself out of this situation by fencing himself off from God somewhat as the fascinating story of the Tower of Babel relates concerning man's effort to climb so high God cannot reach him. He may seek to relieve his situation by the accumulation of this world's goods and the exercise of the power which wealth brings over others. He may attempt to find a way out in a pursuit of wisdom or in a search for power in the world. This is what the prophet Jeremiah is thinking of when he says, "Let not the wise man glory in his wisdom, let not the mighty man glory in his might, let not the rich man glory in his riches; but let him who glories glory in this, that he understands and knows me, that I am the Lord who practices kindness, justice, and righteousness in the earth; for in these things I delight, says the Lord" (Jeremiah 9:23,24). In other words, none of these things can deliver a man—only God alone can do that. One can build his castles in the air, blow his bubbles of escape, bury himself in the pursuit of wealth, wisdom, and power; he can pry deeply into secrets of nature, exploiting her bounties, but all of these things eventually crumble into dust and ashes before his very eyes, unless he becomes re-oriented to God. One of the strongest convictions of Scripture is that all human effort, all human structures of power, and all temporal values are of no avail until man has put God back into the center of his existence. This leads us into the way in which God restores man to his sanity and to fellowship with him.

(4) Man Is Redeemed by God

God comes to us also as our Redeemer. Once one recognizes that he cannot lift himself up by his own boot straps and that his only hope of deliverance from the condition into which sin has brought him lies in the goodness and mercy of God, strange things begin to happen to him. In the cross of Christ one sees God in terms of both judgment and love. In the death of Christ he realizes that Christ "himself bore our sins in his body on the tree, that we might die to sin and live to righteousness" (1 Peter 2:24). His bearing of our sins is in itself an expression of divine judgment upon sin and the sinner. When Peter says further in this same verse "by his wounds you have been healed," we know that divine love is in the foreground. Therefore, as one accepts God's judgment upon him as a sinner and as he responds to God's love for him through Christ he responds to the gift of God's love and in grateful repentance turns from his sins. He starts the movement away from death and condemnation toward a state of life and glory.

What we have said thus far will enable us to see that the human race must pass through three states or stages. There is the integrity man has before sin, his corruption in sin, his redemption from sin and the state of glory when sin is no more. Some Christian thinkers believe that man may find these stages overlapping in his human experience even now. Our Presbyterian belief would certainly say that as Christians there is still corruption in us, we hope that we are being redeemed and that the blessings of redemption we now have are a foretaste of glory.

Suggested Reading:

> *Introduction to the Reformed Tradition*, Chapters III, IV.
> *Call to Faith*, Chapter 4.
> *Confession of Faith*, Chapters 6, 7.
> *Shorter Catechism*, Questions 13–20.
> Scripture, Genesis 3; Psalm 8; Romans 1:18–32; I Corinthians 13.

3.

Our Presbyterian Belief About SIN

Christianity is basically a religion of redemption from sin. This means that sin is at the very center of our Christian idea of salvation. Without sin we would have had no need of a Redeemer. Without sin there would have been no Christianity—a Christian is one who has been redeemed from sin by Christ. Without sin there would have been no Church. Someone has humorously but truthfully said that the Church could no more continue to exist without sin than a supermarket could stay in business without canned goods.

The Christian faith regards sin predominantly in the light of one's relation to God. Even when it is dealing with sin against one's neighbor, it is thinking ultimately of sin against God, and against a human being made in the image of God. Sin is not to be identified with crime, nor should we always equate sin with breaking man-made laws. Sin is essentially a condition of the heart, or an expression of that condition that manifests man's wrong attitudes to God as we shall see later. For instance, in one rendering of the well known hymn by Isaac Watts frequently called "At the Cross," we have these words in the second stanza, "Was it for crimes that I have done, He groaned upon the tree?" It was not for our crimes that Christ has died—it was for our sins. Crimes violate man-made laws, some of which themselves may be wrong. Sins are those things we do that express wrong attitudes toward God.

1. From What Do We Seek Deliverance?

(1) Man Has Been Threatened Differently in History

From time immemorial the individual has felt threatened at the very center of his existence by certain aspects of his experience, facts of life and events in the world before which he has seemed utterly helpless in his own power. In the Old Testament men are crying out unto God for deliverance from such ills as injustice, oppression, and oftentimes from pestilence and famine. When Christianity confronted the Graeco-Roman world men and women were weighed down by the fear and burden of sheer mortality. Even the emperor sometimes had a slave whose chief business was, in the midst of the affairs of daily life, to remind the king that he was but a man and must die. Later, in the time of Augustine who lived in the fifth century, man was seriously concerned because of his deep and ineradicable sense of guilt and the nauseating feeling of corruption. At the time of the Protestant Reformation in the sixteenth century men were deeply concerned as to whether or not they were really saved. They were overcome with a paralyzing fear and a deadening despair. In our modern era, often called the "age of anxiety," men can not endure the sense of the almost utter meaninglessness of life. Nor can they bear up under the ominous possibility of almost instantaneous destruction of our civilization with the unspeakable loss of life which may be involved. Such evils as those above have beset man's existence from the beginning and they are with us today.

(2) The Threat of Death

From what we have just said we may see that redemption in Christ is concerned with more than sin in a narrow sense. It is also concerned with many things which ordinarily we do not regard as sin. They are however basically related to it. More specifically we can say that we are confronted today, as has been true in man's long history, with the basic evils of death, pain, ignorance, and sin. Tertullian taunted the pagan mind of the second and third centuries by saying something like this, "You people who are not Christians could face death calmly and without fear if you knew it to be the end of things for you, but you don't know what is ahead of you and you are all afraid." The Bible has regarded death as man's last enemy, if not his greatest. Serious philosophical thought of our time has pondered much and long over the mystery of death. Without Christ and the hope of his power over death all our thought of death seems to lead down a blind alley.

(3) The Threat of Suffering and Ignorance

Then there is the awful fact of human suffering, some of which is not only repugnant to the human mind, but seems utterly and demoniacally futile. Moreover, so much of it seems, unexplainably, to fall upon the innocent. Here, again, we are not only baffled but "buffaloed" in its presence. Also, we are confronted with the fact of human ignorance and its effect upon the life of the individual and society. While Christianity has never identified sin with ignorance it has always regarded them as inseparably related. It is appalling to recall the evil and suffering that man's ignorance of the natural world has caused in history. Perhaps his ignorance in the moral and spiritual realms is even greater and has brought worse tragedies and bigger catastrophes to the human race.

(4) Sin Is the Basic Evil

However bad and destructive these three evils we have been considering may be, we must confess that the chief evil in our human life is sin. We believe that sin lies behind the evils of death, suffering, and ignorance; that it is the real enemy of mankind and must be overcome at all costs. Ignorance, pain, and even death can be endured with courage, when not overcome, in the light of God's love in the cross of Christ. It is of the essence of our Christian faith to assert that this self-giving divine love in Christ is strong enough to do away with the destructive work of sin.

2. What Is the Significance of the Christian View of Sin?

The Christian doctrine of sin stands over against certain tendencies of our time which have threatened to destroy our western civilization and the basic moral principles upon which much of it has been built. Modern man has attempted to take God out of the center of his existence and to become what is commonly called a "superman." According to this proclivity of human nature man is unwilling to believe that God has any right to limit him; in short, he does not believe there is a God who can limit him. This will to power has given us our Nazi and

Communistic societies. They are the expression of man's egoistic impulses and of his refusal to accept the fact that he is a finite creature. A second tendency of man in the twentieth century has been to submerge man in nature and to regard him as having no value over and above any other thing in nature. This type of thought has led to self-destruction for instead of trying to become God, a human being begins to despair at not having any value at all. Thus like Samson, who "eyeless in Gaza" plunged himself and those around him into an indescribable whirlpool of destruction and death, this tendency leads man to destroy himself—nihilism is the name we give it. To such tendencies the Christian doctrine of sin stands in contrast by telling us that man is only a finite being; that he did not make himself; that the true meaning of life comes from beyond man; and that the goal of man's life is set by the power who made him. These modern tendencies which we have just described are the refusal of man to accept his destiny under God, and to accept God's purpose for him in the world. It is the putting of man's own will ahead of God's will; it is his refusing to accept the control of a higher power and wisdom than his own.

3. Where Is Sin?

(1) Sin Is at the Center of Personality

We believe that sin resides at the very center or core of personal beings. Augustine regarded it as a bent or kink in man's will which caused him to turn away from God and curve in on himself. Sin has often been said to have its seat or center in the will although we must regard it as pervading the entire personality. Our Presbyterian belief has expressed the fact that sin dominates the whole man in the term "total depravity." Of course, this does not mean that everyone who is not a Christian is just as bad as he can be all over but that there is no part of his personality, no thought, word, purpose or deed that is not affected by sin.

(2) Sin Is in the Conscious Mind

Perhaps it will help us to mention the areas in which sin is most easily found in man in the world. There is sin in the conscious mind of man; that is, sin in our lives which we know to exist and to be effective.

All of us know something of our shortcomings and can name many of them. We can be aware of the fact that we harbor envy, hatred, jealousy, pride, greed, and the sins of the flesh in our minds.

(3) Sin Is in the Unconscious Mind

Sin can also take up its abode in the bottom of our mind in what is often spoken of as our "deep mind," or what is more technically called the unconscious mind, that part of our mind of which we are not aware. It is common knowledge today that this compartment of the mind serves as a sort of storehouse for all the things we want to do but are afraid to do, of the unkindly thoughts we have of others but are unwilling to express them. It is generally believed that these things we want to do and for various reasons cannot bring ourselves to do are pushed down into the subterranean caverns of the mind. You might call this the "nest of the nasty," the dwelling of the demonic. For instance, it is said that one may not be able to recall the name of some person disliked very much or may forget an engagement that was regarded as unpleasant. The things that are pushed down into this part of the mind are not so easily gotten rid of and often push towards the level of consciousness. In short, this level of the mind is most dynamic and oftentimes seems to play strange tricks on us. For instance, we may think we love a person when down deep we despise him. The danger is that some day these pent-up feelings may explode and cause a rupture in the relationship. We have stressed both facets of the mind as a place where sin can be found as a means of affirming the old view that sin pervades all of the person.

(4) There Is a Kingdom of Sin in the World

The third area in which we find sin is in the world around us. The evil in society seems to be more than the mere result of individual sin. We believe that once sin gets loose in the world it becomes entwined in everything men do. It is often spoken of as the "kingdom of sin" which is engaged in active opposition to the will of God. It operates beyond the will of the individual to such an extent that the effort of the individual to do anything about it seems futile. Sin thus seems to permeate the economic, social, and political life of the world; it is responsible for evils in our social order and for many of the international misunderstandings which lead to fear, jealousy and hate among the peoples of the world. This "kingdom of sin" seems to receive impetus from an interesting fact stressed by the Communists. It is that when an individual wills to do something that involves relationships with others he is not always able to control the consequences that may ensue. He may will something that in itself is only a small evil but it may turn out to be an evil of great magnitude. Nations have been plunged into wars by some insignificant incident that may have gone unnoticed had not some fortuitous combination of circumstances, unforeseen and certainly unwanted, taken place to turn it into the cause of a major war.

4. What Is Sin?

We come now to consider more specifically the nature of sin. *The Shorter Catechism* says that "Sin is any want of conformity unto, or transgression of, the law of God" (Question 14). This definition has often been criticized as too impersonal and as tending toward legalism. The remark has been made that any Jewish rabbi could have written it. We may admit that as it stands it may sound a bit cold and formal but we may be confident that this was not the intention of those who wrote it. We may be sure that if you could have asked them to sum up the commandments they would have done so by saying that we should love God and our neighbor. For them the relationship of love between God and man was always in the background; obedience to God's will is an expression of love. Christ told his disciples that if they loved him they would keep his commandments. From this standpoint, then, sin is a breach in the personal relationship that man sustains to God. He refuses to do his will or keep his commandments because he does not love him. This enables us to see that sin is really a perverted relationship to God, to our fellowman, to our world, and even to oneself. When the normal relationship between God and man is distorted every other relationship in man's experience becomes discolored. The very fact that one does not love God breeds hostility and this is turned upon others, the world, and oftentimes more especially himself. The first movement of sin then is to make a person a "God-kicker, a God-hater and a God-struggler." He would get rid of God if he could. This is exactly what the demonic forces were trying to do at the cross.

We may say further, therefore, that sin is ultimately a rejection of God's endless and self-giving love in Christ on the cross. It is an expression of his unwillingness to let God love him. Basically, man in sin comes to regard God as thwarting his egoistic and self-centered desires and purposes. Because of this he resents the presence of the divine in the world and wishes God were dead.

5. Where Did Sin Come from?

This is far more than a $64,000 question. The fact is we do not know exactly where sin started. All of us acquainted with the story of fallen man and woman in the garden of Eden. God made us in his own image and without sin. The temptation to sin came from beyond. Why it was that a being who never had known sin and who apparently had no tendency or desire to sin ever did we do not know. We can thus see that the Bible drives sin back beyond the human will, for sin came from the outside. Christianity has never been able to give a precise answer as to how sin got into our world except to say that man to whom God gave freedom of the will voluntarily decided to disobey him. It need not concern us too deeply because we are unable to answer this question, for Christianity is primarily concerned not with explaining either the origin or nature of sin but with doing away with it. It is just as difficult for us to state exactly what place sin holds among the things of the world. We believe that sin is very real but we do not know precisely what sort of reality it is. Is it as real as the human soul? Is it as real as a tree? Or a book? Or a car? Is evil as real as good? God created all things and if evil is as real as they are then God would be the author of evil. Our Presbyterian theologians have often discussed this question but have never been able to give a thoroughly satisfactory answer. It is often said that sin is real morally and logically but that it is not real in the sense in which these other things are.

6. What Kinds of Sin Are There?

There are many ways in which sins can be classified. We usually speak of sins of the flesh as over against sins of the spirit. The former are more obvious and we have frequently stressed them to the neglect of the sins of the Spirit. Jesus had much more to say against pride, hate, covetousness, and the desire for revenge than he did about drunkenness and even crasser forms of debauchery. He was confronted by sins of the spirit in his contacts with the religious leaders. Their pride and self-righteousness made it impossible for them to have an openness of mind and spirit toward him and his message. They felt they had no need of his help and turned away from him in proud disgust. His experience with those who had been ravaged by the sins of the flesh was different. He seemed to mingle easily and naturally, as well as helpfully, with sinners, publicans, and even harlots. The reason for this seems to be that the sins of the Spirit had so closed the minds of the religious leaders to any sense of spiritual need. Did they not have their position, their education, their wealth, and their good deeds? They were not dependent upon him to enrich their lives. But what could the sinners, the publicans, and the harlots depend upon? They were truly the poor in spirit. Both Calvin and Luther make mention of the fact that these sins of the Spirit shut out of the kingdom those who were most ardently devoted to the cause of religion, but that those who were utterly dependent upon God's grace and goodness entered into it, though unworthy.

7. How Does Sin Express Itself?

We have seen the various sins that enter our lives and tend to destroy us. These sins are common to our human nature and we see them creeping out in one way or another in every generation. We should not, however, come to believe that the manifestations of sin are exactly the same in every age or culture. Our human life and personality are profoundly affected by the social matrix in which we have been placed by Divine Providence. In a culture based upon slavery those who are enslaved would be affected differently in their attitudes and responses in the realm of human relationships than those who are free. We cannot imagine the resentments, hatreds, and tensions that can arise within the heart of a man who is treated as an inferior and as a means to an end by other persons. Nor are we able to estimate the damage done to the character and personality of men and women who habitually and instinctively consider themselves as superior to other segments of humanity and who come to feel that they have an inherent right to use them as the means of fulfilling their own desires and purposes. We are conscious today of the many ills that have befallen human personality because of the type of culture we have developed in western society. It is true that we have only begun to understand why it is there are so many sick persons as a result of our way of life. Such things as crime, divorce, murder, alcoholism, drug addiction, and juvenile delinquency, not to mention suicide, are intimately bound up with the whole problem of sin in a man's relation to his neighbor and to his world in our twentieth century culture.

It may not be as easy for us to deal with the complexities of human nature as it was for our forefathers who could call most anything they didn't like sin. It remains true, however, that when we get to the bottom of the "neurotic personalities" of our time, sin in some fashion or other will be crouching at the door. Christian ministers have often been criticized because they can see only one thing wrong with human nature and only one cure for it. Some of us are willing to confess that we cannot say glibly, "Jesus is the answer." Nor can we say too lightly that if we accept Christ all our troubles will be at an end. Of course this depends upon what we mean. The experience on the Damascus road was only the beginning of trials, troubles, and tribulations for Paul. The Christian minister can attempt so to portray Christ, the only entirely whole personality known to us, that others may see him as he is and want to become like him. When this happens we are on the road to the discovery of a way to cope with sin.

Suggested Reading:

Call to Faith, Chapter 6.
Confession of Faith, Chapters 6, 7.
Shorter Catechism, Questions 13–16.
Scripture, Genesis 1, 2; Psalm 51; Mark 7:14–23; Romans 7.

4.

Our Presbyterian Belief About GRACE (or Redemption)

In our Christian faith we are naturally led to think of grace, once the fact of sin confronts us. This is because the bestowal of God's grace is his way of offsetting and overcoming the effects and power of sin in human life, and in the world. When we come to the study of the grace of God we are right up against the tremendous doctrine of redemption. Thus it makes little difference whether we speak of grace, of redemption, of salvation, of forgiveness, or of eternal life, for these realities are so intimately bound together in the New Testament that you cannot think of one without the other.

Martin Luther had a unique way of speaking concerning the blessings that come to us from the grace of God as a result of the redemptive work of Christ. He put it like this: God gives us Jesus Christ and when we, through faith, accept him there come to us all the mercies, or blessings that Christ has provided by his death and Resurrection. He goes on to say that, once we have received Christ there are given to us faith, and the Holy Spirit who creatively works in us to bring forth all the rich fruits of Christian experience. Consequently, we could as easily have used the title "The Holy Spirit" for our chapter heading, as any other. The thought is that all the work of grace, or all the blessings of redemption, or to put it another way, every fulfillment of God's promises in Christ, are the work of the Holy Spirit. We shall return to this aspect of our belief when we consider the Christian life, for just as everything in our salvation depends upon the Holy Spirit in the initial work of salvation, the entire Christian life which follows is also the result of his creative power.

1. Where Do We Find the Promise of God's Grace?

(1) God Seeks Man

The story of God's redemptive love or his gracious activity in behalf of humanity is set forth in the Bible alone. Christianity is different from every other religion in that it conceives God as seeking man, while other religions regard man as seeking and finding God. The expression is seen to follow closely upon the fact of man's falling into sin. It has been pointed out, for instance, that the story of the first sin also contains an account of God's care and concern for man in holding out to him a way of escape from the power of sin. Also, while Cain is banished from his own people because of the murder of his brother Abel, he is also marked in such a way as to set him apart as one for whom God cares, and therefore he is not to be harmed. Furthermore, the devastating flood in the time of Noah does not harm his family to whom God's grace has been shown. In each of these instances of failure due to sin God manifests his grace by holding out hope for the future.

(2) God's Grace Is to Be Universal

When we come to the story of the Tower of Babel the statement just made seems not to hold true. Nothing is said in this account concerning any specific way of deliverance from the awful confusion and chaos which human pride and arrogance produced. But it is just at this point that something occurs which enables us to see that God's grace is not only at work, but that his redemptive purpose for mankind is taking on a much broader scope. In the very same chapter in which the tragic event at Babel is recorded we have the beginning of the story of Abraham to whom God's grace is going to be given with the express purpose of its eventually reaching the whole human race. "And I will make of you a great nation, and I will bless you, and make your name great, so that you will be a blessing. I will bless those who bless you, and him who curses you I will curse; and by you all the families of the earth shall bless themselves" (Genesis 12:2–3).

(3) God's Grace Is Seen in the Whole Bible

It is our Presbyterian belief that God's promise of grace to and through Abraham is being fulfilled throughout the whole of the Old Testament and reaches its highest and final fulfillment in Christ. We believe that even the law of Moses is set in the framework of grace, and that it points eventually to the redemptive work of Christ, who is the "end of the law." It should be noted, in this connection, that the Ten Commandments are prefaced by a statement reminding Israel of God's deliverance from Egypt: "I am the Lord your God, who brought you out of the land of Egypt, out of the house of bondage" (Exodus 20:2). This passage of Scripture is what *The Shorter Catechism* calls the "Preface" to the Ten Commandments, and in order to see its full significance we should think of it as coming before each of the Ten Commandments. In other words, every one of the Ten Commandments is properly introduced by recalling to mind God's gracious work of redemption for Israel. If then, we were considering the Ten Commandments from a Christian point of view a similar expression of God's grace in Christ would serve as an appropriate preface. We could say, for example, I am the Lord thy God who has delivered you from your sins and brought you redemption through Jesus Christ. Thus it is God's gracious activity in Christ that provides the motive for our endeavoring to live according to the will of God as given us in the Ten Commandments. The New Testament gives us the story of the highest and final fulfillment of God's promise of grace in Christ. The Christian Church, as the body of Christ, is itself the gift of God's grace, and the bearer of the message of his redemptive purpose, or grace, in the Old and New Testaments.

Jeremiah points to the time of a new covenant: "Behold, the days come, saith the Lord, that I will make a new covenant with the house of Israel, and with the house of Judah. Not according to the covenant that I made with their fathers in the day that I took them by the hand to bring them out of the Land of Egypt; which my covenant they brake, although I was an husband unto them, said the Lord" (Jeremiah

31:31–32 paraphrased). When Jesus instituted the Sacrament of the Lord's Supper, he said of the cup, "This cup is the New Covenant in my blood" (1 Cor. 11:25). We believe he is thinking here of the promise of the new covenant made by Jeremiah centuries earlier. There are several places in the New Testament that mention the covenant promise by Jeremiah as being fulfilled through Christ in the Christian Church. By this time we should begin to see that grace, or redemption, is God's answer to the universal sin of mankind, and to his failure to live in fellowship with God. The Bible is the story of God's gracious effort to save the human race from its own folly.

2. What Do We Mean by Redemption?

Often we take the meaning of such words as grace and redemption for granted; although we may find it hard to state specifically what they do mean. We can say that grace is God's loving attempt to save a person from the guilt, power, and effects of his sinful nature. Central to the meaning of grace is the idea that man in no way deserves or merits what God does for him in redemption. It has as an essential notion the thought of making whole again. Life, as a result of sin, has become shot through and through with all kinds of contradictions. His inner life has been broken into bits, or pieces. Sin has left a split or cleft at the very core of his personality. God's grace in redemption is at work restoring wholeness, completeness, and fullness. This is possible because the self, which has been placed at the center of his existence and which has caused the fragmentation of his inner life, thrusting the scattered segments of the self in all directions, gives way to God in Christ who brings together his inner self and heals the soul's brokenness.

(1) The Image of God Is Restored

It is possible for us to say that redemption means several different things, all of which are intimately bound together in our lives. First, once we have accepted Christ in faith and depend upon him alone for our salvation, the Holy Spirit begins to restore the image of God in us which was broken and marred by sin. We begin a new kind of life at the center of our being which makes once more for wholeness, and which moves away from sin and death towards God and life. We begin to take on the character God intended us to have when he created humanity. There is produced in character and life, by the creative work of the Spirit, those qualities we would have possessed had not sin sidetracked us. We could say that redemption is the operation of God's grace in life which enables us to live more nearly in accord with the will of God, and to express in life those graces which so abundantly adorned the life of our Lord.

(2) Inner Unity Is Restored

The second thing that happens to us in redemption is that our lost inner unity and integrity are restored. As mentioned above, once God enters the central chamber of our being, and we give him control at the very core of our existence, our inner contradictions are reduced, and the broken pieces of selfhood are united and brought together by the central drive of our will to live in harmony with the will of God. We are told by psychologists, almost on every hand today, that this inner splitness of human personality cannot be overcome in one's own strength, there has to be some outside help. Many examples could be given to show that men who were confused, frustrated, and overwhelmed by this lack of inner unity found wholeness in Christ and were enabled to make lasting contributions to history. Paul is certainly one man who was torn asunder inside himself until Jesus confronted him on the Damascus road. After that experience, however, he became one of the world's most energetic and constructive figures whose lifelong slogan was, "This one thing I do." The same thing could be said for Augustine, who was a weak, vacillating, debauched man until he read of the promise of God's grace in Christ. Then the pieces of his inner life began to come together, and through sheer force of character, thought, and life, he helped to hold together Western civilization for a thousand years. John Calvin, Martin Luther, John Wesley, and almost countless others bear a similar testimony to the power of God's grace to restore inner unity to the human soul.

(3) We Are Restored to Fellowship with God and Neighbor

A third blessing that comes to us in redemption is the fact that God restores us to fellowship with himself, and with our neighbor. We have seen that sin tears us away from God, and isolates us from mankind.

Our human life becomes a constant movement away from God and our human relations become opportunities of oppression and exploitation of our fellowman. But once one accepts God's love for him as expressed in the cross of Christ and realizes that because of what God has done for him in Christ, he need no longer look upon his creator as his enemy—he can have peace with God. So long as man feels that what he is doing is out of harmony with God's will, and that the rest of his life is moving away from God, he will have attitudes of pride, rebellion, and hostility. These are not only directed toward God but toward his neighbor. But let a person come to realize that God really loves him—which is the central meaning of the cross—he not only can enter again into fellowship with God, but he can also enter into wholesome, unselfish, and positive relations with his neighbor.

(4) Man's Control of Nature Is Restored

We can say that there is also a fourth element in man's redemption. Our Presbyterian belief has generally held that one aspect of the image of God in man may be seen in the fact that God gave him dominion over the world (Psalm 8). We believe that it was God's intention for man to use all the bounties of the world for his own welfare, subject to the principle that his use of the abundance of nature would always be for the glory of God. Historians have given John Calvin some credit for the advance of our scientific knowledge concerning nature in that he held to the notion just mentioned above. Man's sin has made it impossible for him to use the gifts and the powers of the natural world either for the highest welfare of mankind, or for the ultimate glory of God. Therefore, he not only exploits his neighbor, but he exploits nature. While he is still able to exercise a certain type of control over the world his unwise use of the bounties of nature, in the long run, turn back upon him in destruction and death. All of us know that this is no mere fancy nor idle tale in the twentieth century. It is a basic Christian conviction that a man, whose life is surrendered to the will of God, could handle the affairs of our world and use the products of nature far more wisely than man without any regard for God is ever able to do.

(5) Man Regains His True Destiny

The final aspect of redemption to be mentioned here is that a person has restored to him his true destiny. There is inside the being of every one of us an insatiable drive towards some goal, some fulfillment, which our experience teaches us we all fall short of. It is not only that we "fall short of the glory of God," but we do not come up to the potentialities of the human self. What we are thinking of here pertains primarily to this life, but it definitely includes our thought of man's entire destiny. We cannot separate man's ultimate destiny from the meaning and goal of his earthly life. As we shall see later the quality of life that comes to us in Christ is such that it begins in us that fulfillment that reaches its final goal only in the life to come. We can say that God intended that our destiny in this life be far greater than what it is for us in sin, and that he intended our ultimate destiny to be eternal fellowship with him. Because of this we can confidently assert in faith that God does restore to us our true destiny both in this life and in the life to come. All of this is the work of grace.

3. How Do We Get God's Grace?

(1) Grace Is Through the Cross

We have seen some of the things that happen to us in redemption. We come now, to the question, How is it that these blessings of redemption, of which we have spoken, become ours? The very backbone of our Christian faith is seen in the atoning work of Christ on the cross. It does not make very much difference how we express it so long as we point to the same reality—the fact that he bore our sins on the cross. In his death he did for us what we could in nowise do for ourselves as in his life he lived as no man has ever been able to live. Thus we see that God's love is ever self-giving, but that at the same time God's justice is but the other side of his love. This is true because God himself, in Christ, does for man what under the law man had never been able to do in his own power. This tremendous truth overwhelms us every time we hear the words of the first and last stanzas of "When I Survey the Wondrous Cross,"

> When I survey the wondrous cross,
> On which the Prince of Glory died,
> My richest gain I count but loss,
> And pour contempt on all my pride.

Were the whole realm of nature mine,
That were a present far too small;
Love so amazing, so divine,
Demands my soul, my life, my all.

(2) Redemption Comes Through Faith

Everything that God does for us through his grace comes to us through faith. This is one of the greatest words in the language of the New Testament. Faith itself is a gift of the Holy Spirit. We have always been taught that the Holy Spirit is a light-giving power. This enables us to say that when the Holy Spirit enters our life he throws a new light upon the mind which enables us to see things we had not seen or known. For instance his gift of faith brings to us the realization that what Christ has done on the cross can be made our very own. Faith enables us to know what we had refused to believe before, that if there is any hope for us in our sins it is in what Christ has done for us. That is, "we receive and rest upon him alone for salvation."

The work of faith, once it comes to us, is to accept what Christ has done for us; although we know we are not worthy of the benefits he brings to us in redemption. Faith is, in a sense, believing something that is too good to be true—that God forgives us freely when we are still sinful. It has always been hard for man to believe that God can and will accept him as he is, or that God can and will save him without his contributing something to his salvation. Because of this all sorts of legalism have ever threatened the Christian faith. Some one has said that in faith we accept the fact that God accepts us, although we know we are not acceptable to him. This is indeed faith. It is through this kind of faith we are redeemed because we are willing to receive what God has done for us in Christ. We should remember that we are saved through faith rather than by faith, for it is not actually our faith that saves us, but Christ!

(3) The Place of Repentance in Redemption

Repentance has often been called a twin grace of faith. Both of them are regarded as belonging together, and as equally the gifts of the Holy Spirit. It means primarily to turn back to God upon realization of the hopelessness of the path of sin, and of the hopefulness of the way of life in Christ. It means literally a change of mind after thought, it means the turning around from the direction in which we are going when the tragedy and futility of that course are disclosed, and a better way is offered in Christ.

We can say that another thing happens in repentance. A tremendous change takes place at the center of our existence. Self, as the center of life, is replaced by God in Christ. This means that everything in life will be looked upon from an entirely new point of view, or perspective. Instead of our life remaining self-centered, there is the effort to make it God-centered, or Christ-centered, so that we may say, "For to me to live is Christ" (Philippians 1:21). A new power of control takes over in the inmost chamber of our person, and everything that follows in life is subject to a new center of gravity. The fact should be stressed, as was done by the Reformers, that repentance is not something that happens at the very beginning of our Christian experience, and is over with once and for all. In the broad sense, in which we are looking at it, repentance really goes along with the whole process of Christian growth, through all of life. This is brought out in *The Shorter Catechism* definition of sanctification which tells us, "It is the work of God's free grace, whereby we are renewed in the whole man after the image of God, and are enabled more and more to die unto sin, and live unto righteousness" (Question 35).

Suggested Reading:

Introduction to the Reformed Tradition, Chapter IV.
Call to Faith, Chapter 7.
Confession of Faith, Chapters 9, 10.
Shorter Catechism, Questions 29–35.
Scripture, Romans 8–11; Ephesians 2, 3.

5.

Our Presbyterian Belief About the SCRIPTURES

At this point one may well ask, how can we know that all the things we have been thinking about thus far are true? Where do we go to find out the truth about God, man, sin, and grace, as well as the other aspects of the Christian faith? During the time of the Protestant Reformation the Church really held to three sources of religious truth, the Bible, tradition, and the teachings of the Church. This view made room for all sorts of egregious errors, some of which had already crept into the Church's doctrine and practice. The leaders of the Reformation held that the Bible alone is our source of religious authority and truth. Both John Calvin and Martin Luther were very emphatic in giving the Scriptures first place as our source of knowledge in the Christian faith. Since that time it has been an essential part of our Protestant, and especially of our Reformed, heritage to regard the Bible as our only certain rule for faith and practice. There were minor differences in the views of Calvin and Luther but they stood together in this conviction about the Word of God.

They believed every Christian should have the right of free access to the Scriptures, and both of them were founders of an educational system that was designed to equip men and women to read and understand the Scriptures. Students from practically all over Europe flocked to Geneva for the purpose of sitting at the feet of the great interpreters of the Bible under John Calvin's direction. With the Bible in their hands, and its truth impressed upon their hearts, they went all over Europe and the British Isles proclaiming the good news of the gospel truths as set forth in Scriptures. A statue in Geneva showing some of the leading Reformers during and shortly after the Reformation depicts each one according to the particular emphasis of his life's work. John Calvin is shown with both his hands on the Bible indicating that whatever he did, whether teaching, preaching, writing or administering the affairs of church and state, it was based upon the teaching of Scripture.

1. How Do We Know There Is a God?

(1) All Men Know There Is a God

We have already seen from Chapter One that the question "Is there a God?" sounds almost absurd, according to one of our leading present day thinkers. The reason it is thought to be a foolish query is because the existence of God is regarded as known by every man. From the time of Augustine, there have been those who have held that man cannot even know himself as a self-conscious being without realizing that there is a God. They have said that when one comes to know himself he also knows the world around him, and that both himself and the world are derived from some source or power beyond themselves. In short, we cannot come to know anything at all about ourselves, or about our world, without knowing it in God. Everything we know, think, or experience is known, thought, and experienced in him. There seems to be imbedded in the very structure of the human mind the ability to apprehend that there is a God. Most of us have heard it stated that Helen Keller has remarked that a long time before anyone ever told her about God she had thought of him. This is what we might call "built-in" knowledge of God.

(2) Men Believe in God Because of the World

Others have come to believe that there is a God as they have reflected upon their experience in and of the world in which we live. It is difficult for us to believe that such a vast, magnificent universe as this has come into being accidentally, or of itself. Some years ago there were scientists who seemed to think that it was reasonable to believe that a million monkeys, writing on as many typewriters, for millions of years, would eventually hit off all the Shakesperian plays and sonnets, or perhaps such a book as the Bible. They went on to indicate that our world may have come into being in such an accidental fashion. I think we will agree that such a view demands greater credulity from the human mind than the Christian doctrine of creation. People have been led to believe in God when they have observed the order and regularity of the physical universe, and as they have found in the development of nature signs of purposive movement toward foreseen goals. Further, some have believed that there is a God because of the evidences of the moral order which expresses itself in and through the human conscience. What we have been saying leads us to see that man cannot think upon the world around him, or step out into that world, or think about his own inner life without being confronted with the fact that there is a God. We can admit, therefore, that it would seem to take even a greater faith to reject a belief in the existence of God than it would to accept it. But actually the big question for Christian faith is not the existence of God. It is "What is God like?" None of the above considerations can really answer this.

2. Where Do We Learn What God Is Like?

(1) Christ Is God's Word

As Christians, the real question is "Who is God?" rather than "Is there a God?" "What is God like for me?" rather than "What is God like in himself?" This is the starting point for Christian thought. And this question finds an answer only in Revelation. It is Scripture alone that tells us what God's attitude toward sinful man is, and what God's purpose for mankind is. As we have seen, the revelation of his purpose began in the early portions of the Old Testament. We will now consider this more fully. The prophets and the apostles are all saying the same thing—they are repeating over and over the statement that God is gracious, God is loving, God is forgiving, and God is redeeming. Each prophet is pointing forward to Christ, and each apostle is pointing back to him. This is because the one great word all of them uttered tells of

God's seeking and self-giving love to mankind. When at last God himself came to the people in Christ, the Good Shepherd, we know that he has spoken his final Word. This is why every writer, prophet, and apostle in Scripture is pointing to this expression of God's love, and it is the core of the Messianic element in the Old Testament. In Christ, who is the way, the truth, and the life we can be sure of God's love. Christ is God's Word for man. He discloses God's purpose for mankind; he is the embodiment of the Father's redeeming love. He is the final revelation of God's own being in our midst. Christ is the living Word of God.

(2) Christ Is the Bridge Between God and Man

When we speak of Christ as the Word of God we mean that he tells us all there is to know about God's attitude toward us. A word in our language forms a bridge between two minds. Christ as the Word brings God and man together and whether we say Christ, salvation, redemption, or forgiveness, they are all words of love which help to bridge the chasm that sin has put between God and man. The only thing that God can offer us in our sinfulness is his love, and we believe that the only way in which he could offer his love is in Christ.

All of the promises God has ever made have been of grace. They have all expressed his love, and they have all been fulfilled in Christ. The love of God as manifest in Christ is the only thing that can cure our sin. Or, we may say, the one great need of our human life is love. God in Christ does what he can do for man—he gives him his love. Man in Christ receives all he needs—that is love. So the Word of God in Christ brings God and man together, who had been torn apart from each other by sin. Christ is the Word—the bridge.

(3) Christ Is the Living Word

The great aim of the Scriptures is to make the Word stand out and live for us, to get hold of us and change our lives. The entire Bible is the Word of God, and the theme of the whole is redemption. But the great word God has to utter for mankind is redemption. And, as Luther said, even when we are using our own words, if we proclaim Christ as redeemer, that is, in a true sense, the Word of God. To refer to the great Reformers once more, they thought Christ as set forth in the

Scripture is the Living Word, and that it was our duty in the Church so to present him that men could behold him in all of his redemptive power. That is why Calvin said the community that portrays Christ with the least obscurity is the true Church. When we hear the Scripture read from the pulpit, or when we read it in private, Christ is seen to rise up from its very pages and speak to us the redeeming and commanding words such as: "Follow me," or "Come unto me all you who labor and are heavy laden." That is, by the power of the Spirit, he rises up before us and challenges us as though he were actually confronting us physically.

3. How Do We Know That the Scriptures Give Us the Word of God?

We have seen that the prophets really gave us the voice of God, and that in Christ we find God coming to us expressing in a personal being his word of redemption and love. We believe, then, that the Scriptures present the Word of God to us because this is the only place man ever hears the call to accept the redemptive love of God. No place else do we hear that prophetic voice offering redemptive love to man, and no place else do we see that person who embodies redemptive love as we find it in Christ. The Scriptures alone give us this inspired record of the revelation of divine love. Here alone do we have the only real knowledge of God in the strictly Christian sense. The Bible alone tells us how we can enter into fellowship with Him after having broken that relationship. As the Catechism says, the Word of God, "which is contained in the Scriptures of the Old and New Testaments, is the only rule to direct us how we may glorify and enjoy him" (Question 2). We can neither glorify nor enjoy God until we know that he has spoken to us his unchanging word of love, and for that reason the next question in the Catechism tells us that Scripture teaches, "What man is to believe concerning God, and what duty God requires of man" (Question 3). Perhaps if we were writing this last statement today we could express it more clearly that the Scripture teaches us what we are to believe concerning God's attitude toward us in Christ. For once we know this, we go on in Scripture to learn what our attitude toward God should be. We can readily see, then, that as God has so endlessly and unchangingly loved us, our response to that love should be one of willing and cheerful obedience to his will. "If you love me, you will keep my commandments" (John 14:15). This is the mainspring of all Christian conduct and service.

4. In What Sense Is the Scripture the Guide of Life?

(1) Christ Is Our Example

The Bible is not a book of magic, nor does it contain a set of hard and fast rules. It presents us first, with a picture of the kind of persons God wants us to be. This is true even in the Old Testament where we find commandments and specific rules for living often set out in exact detail. It is even truer in the New Testament in which men and women are constantly being encouraged to live the Christian life at its best. The Church has always seen in Christ a pattern, or an example for Christian living. We are often encouraged to love as he did, to have the mind in us that Christ had, and to show patience in suffering and in trouble as he manifested in his early ministry. Christians are urged to forgive one another as they have been forgiven by Christ. Several qualities are characteristic of the early Christian Church. It is a community which seems to be more conscious of God than of any other reality. It is marked by a generous, unselfish, Christian love. There is a sense of absolute dependence upon God in all things. Simplicity of life prevails as an ideal—and for the most part as a practice. Such virtues as faith, hope, meekness, humility, and longsuffering are continually held before the early Christians for their encouragement to richer and more abundant living.

(2) Love Is the Basic Principle of Life

The basic principle that seems to govern all of life for the New Testament writers is that of love. In the Old Testament love and justice for neighbor go hand in hand. In these two simple words it is possible to sum up the moral teachings of the Old Testament. Micah expresses this for us, "He has showed you, O man, what is good; and what does the Lord require of you, but to do justice, and to love kindness, and to walk humbly with your God" (Micah 6:8). Our Lord emphatically confirms this Old Testament conviction in what we, perhaps too sentimentally, call the Golden Rule. He says, "So whatsoever you wish that men would do to you, do so to them; for this is the law and the prophets" (Matthew 7: 12). It is interesting to note that Jesus says on this principle of love hangs all the law and the prophets. Love is the law of the Kingdom of God; it is the highest expression of the indwelling power of the Holy Spirit in a person's life. It is the fulfillment of the law of the Old Testament, and the fullest expression of the grace of Christ in our life in the New. Certainly in the places in which the Bible speaks of our various human relationships it is understood that love is the foremost and basic principle.

(3) The Bible Sets Forth the Meaning of Life

The Bible also sets forth for us the true meaning and purpose of human existence. It has been said that the temptation of our Lord on the Mount contains all the meaning of human history, and that the three questions put to him in his temptation give us a true insight into the meaning and purpose of life. Would he live his life in such a way as to bind people to him through his power over their physical life? Would he exploit their credulity and gullibility by forcing them into a state of childlike awe and wonder at the marvelous powers of his personality? Would he coerce men into following him through sheer exercise of power? Or would he pursue his destined way to the cross, and fulfill his Messianic role in loving obedience to God, and in sacrifical service to mankind? From the first utterance in response to the temptation, "Man shall not live by bread alone," we know that he has seen to the very depths of God's purpose for him, and for all mankind.

A few years ago a young man stood on the ledge of a New York skyscraper, with the intention of plunging to sudden death below. Newspaper reports told of frantic efforts on the part of officers and bystanders to persuade him not to jump. All such endeavors seemed completely futile. Finally, after one of the persons present urged him to turn back from this tragic ending of his life the young man turned to him in a spirit, and with a look of utter defiance, he asked, "Can you give me one good reason to go on living?" It is difficult for us to conceive of such an answer being given without in some way being related to the purpose of human life as described in Scripture.

5. What About the Bible Today?

As Presbyterians the Bible has been one of our most precious heritages from the past. Our ancestors have loved it, studied it, taught it, preached it, and tried to live by it. But we may well ask as we draw our study of the Scriptures to a close, "Is the Bible relevant today?" "Is it as important for us to know and understand the Bible as it was for Christians in the past?" Perhaps another form of the question would be something like this, "With all of our modern knowledge in the fields of science, psychology, philosophy, and sociology, is it not a bit old-fashioned to hold on to the Bible?" "Is the Bible not out of date in this age of atomic energy and of recent discoveries concerning outer space?" To all of these questions we must give an emphatic No, because the Bible is, in a real sense, a timeless book. It is a book for all times, and for every age. This is because it deals with the unchanging need of the human spirit for forgiveness, understanding, fellowship, faith, hope and love. The Bible speaks to those fears of our human existence that lie at the deeper portions of our being. The Bible addresses itself to our deepest human concerns, anxieties, dreams, hopes and aspirations.

Science can tell us how many tons of material are pouring into our universe each second. It can measure with uncanny accuracy the distance of the remotest stars and planets, giving us their size and probable weight. It can outline with great precision their course in space. But it cannot measure the depth nor weight of the burden of human guilt that presses the human soul. Science can tell us nothing of that awful inner pain and anguish that can come to the human heart that has no light, no hope, no love, and knows only night, darkness, snow and cold. Science can analyze the physical life of an anxious woman bending over the bed of a feverish child, it may even tell us what the chemical elements are in the tears that stream down her face. It can mark every movement of her body, but it cannot measure her anxiety nor weigh the grief that seems to be splitting her heart. Nor can science answer the question asked long ago, "If a man die shall he live again?", although it may lengthen the span of his life. Questions like these belong to the realm of the Spirit. They express the agony and the anguish of human souls, and in this "Age of Anxiety" we can say as Peter did in the long ago when our Lord asked of his disciples, "Will you also go away?" Peter's reply was "Lord, to whom shall we go? You have the words of eternal life" (John 6:68). For this reason there will always be a Bible.

Suggested Reading:

Introduction to the Reformed Tradition, Chapters I, V, VI.
Call to Faith, Chapter 3.
Confession of Faith, Chapter 1.
Shorter Catechism, Questions 2, 3.
Scripture, Psalm 19:7–11; Matthew 5:17–19; John 1:1–14; John 5:39; 2 Timothy 3:16, 17.

6.

Our Presbyterian Belief About CHRIST

Often the remark has been made that one of the main differences between John Calvin and Martin Luther was that Calvin began his theological thinking with the idea of the sovereignty of God and Luther started with the experience of salvation through faith in Christ. While there may be some truth in this contrast between the two great leaders, it can be truthfully said that Calvin has as much to say about the centrality of Christ in Christian experience as any other writer in the field of Christian thought. His chief opposition to the Roman Catholicism of his day was that by its clericalism, stress upon the Sacraments as necessary to salvation, and elevation of the Church to such an exalted position it was shutting the people off from Jesus Christ by shoving him into the background. This was equally true of the tendency which was very strong at that time to think of the Virgin Mary as being closer to the worshipper, as having a more gentle disposition, and as being more merciful than Christ. Calvin could not tolerate anything in the Christian faith that separated the believer from his Lord, or reduced the role Christ fulfilled as our Saviour.

We have seen above that God in Christ utters his one great word of love. The New Testament enables us to catch the full meaning of the fact that Christ discloses to us God's attitude toward man in the term "the grace of Christ." It was especially this truth about Christ's person and work which Calvin stressed in his writing, teaching, and preaching. He followed Luther in saying we could regard the Scriptures as giving us both Law and gospel. For Calvin even the Law ultimately points us to Christ and he is the full embodiment of the gospel. That is, wherever we find Christ in the Bible it is as if we were looking at the "smile of God." If we think of God's will in Christ, Calvin said we could simply write the word "love" instead of will—for his will is his "love toward us." "And the Word became flesh and dwelt among us, full of grace and truth." (John 1:14)

1. Why Is Christ So Important to Us?

(1) The Impression Christ Makes

When we read the gospels we are impressed with two facts about our Lord. First, we see there is in and about him an element of mystery which we sense in no other person we know or about whom we have read. We realize there is something about him that is over and above anything we find in other great personalities. Those who saw and heard him in the gospel stories were aware of this mysterious quality of his character and person. Then, too, when people gathered around him, saw him do the gracious works of his ministry, heard him speak to them about the deeper realities of life they either believed and followed him or rejected and turned away. We wonder why it was that nearly always these two responses toward him were a part of the experience of those who knew him—they wondered and they decided either for or against him.

(2) What Christ Has Done

Christ is important for us because of what he did for us by his life, death and resurrection. *The Shorter Catechism* gives us one of the best statements of his person and work we can find anywhere. "The only Redeemer of God's elect is the Lord Jesus Christ, who being the eternal Son of God, became man, and so was, and continueth to be God and man, in two distinct natures, and one person forever" (Question 21). Yet this description of our Lord shows us very clearly something of the tremendous mystery we face in thinking of his incarnation, that is, of taking human form as the Son of God. We may well ask how can our puny minds explain how God became man in Christ? Of course, they cannot, but our Christian faith has always insisted he did just that and it goes on to say he did it for our deliverance from sin.

(3) Man Cannot Explain Christ

Because of the difficulty of understanding how the incarnation could take place, the person of Christ has been the subject of long and bitter controversies. No less than six Church Councils were called as a result of the disputes that arose concerning the nature of Christ. Six creeds were written before the Church was satisfied that this difficult question had been adequately dealt with in Christian thought. It is interesting to note, however, that the writers of the creeds never really tried to explain the person of Jesus Christ or to tell how the two natures came together to form one person. What they tried to do was to say that human speculation and theories about Christ can go so far but no farther. They are somewhat like a guard; they protect the central truth that he is but one person with two natures. When we go too far in our efforts to explain his person they say you must stop here.

2. Is Christ Both God and Man?

(1) He Must Be Divine

Our Christian faith has always asserted Christ is both God and man. This view alone can do justice to what the Bible says about the nature of our Lord's person. There is another reason why the men who wrote our creeds have so stubbornly held to the belief that he is both God and man. They felt that if he was not truly and fully both divine and human our salvation was in jeopardy. They wanted to preserve the reality and integrity of our Redemption in Christ. The salvation of mankind in and through Christ does stand in danger if he is not both God and man and we do not want to be in doubt as to the validity of our salvation. We must regard him as divine so he can lift us out of the situation of sin. If he were merely human, he would be subject to sin as we are, and one who is in the same predicament—that is, of sin—cannot help others out of it. He must, therefore, come from beyond the conditions of our human life and its sinful tendencies if he is to be able to rescue

us. As one of the religious writers of a century ago has said, if Christ
was guilty of even the smallest sin he could not be our Saviour from
sin. He had to be without sin to save us. If he is not divine, then he is
only a creature in time, space, and history as we are. We can be redeemed from sin only by a power that comes from beyond us.

(2) He Must Also Be Human

It is equally important that we consider Christ as being fully human,
a true man. If he is not as human as we are, he could not represent us
in the flesh and the deeds he did were not the works of a human being,
but of some superhuman person. It has always been the teaching of our
Church that you cannot make him too human but it is a serious mistake
to think of him as merely human. Some historians have said there have
been more theories that have denied the true humanity of Christ than
there have been that have denied his divinity. As Presbyterians we can
take great pride in the fact that John Calvin went to great length to
prove the full and true humanity of Christ, so much so that he was
accused of detracting from the Divinity of our Lord. This was of course
untrue. But in the great controversies, during the Protestant Reformation and after, concerning the presence of Christ in the Sacrament of
the Lord's Supper, Calvin argued unwaveringly for his true and perfect
humanity which made it impossible for him to accept either the Roman
Catholic or Lutheran view of the Sacrament.

3. Why Can We Say Christ Is Unique?

(1) All Cannot Accept Christ Today

To those of us brought up on the Christian Church the uniqueness
of Christ's person and work may be taken for granted. This is not so
for vast numbers of people today who have little, if any, instruction in
the Christian faith or contact with the Church. Christ often presents a
difficulty to the modern mind because generations of critical study and
scientific knowledge have helped to deaden our sense of realities that
belong to the dimension of life dealt with by Christian faith. The ar-
guments we mentioned above in the early centuries of Christianity were
what some one has called "estimates of faith." Many of the views of
our time with reference to Christ are "estimates of unbelief." Or perhaps of doubt. We may ask the question, then, why do we continue to

hold on to our claims for Christ as the final and deepest answer to our greatest human needs? Why, we may ask, in a world like ours, do we Christians continue to hold on to him as our greatest source of hope and faith in life?

(2) Christ Makes Unique Claims for Himself

When we turn to the New Testament we are confronted with the towering figure of a person who, as noted earlier, seems always to be surrounded by an element of mystery and who "haunts" us with His demands upon us until we either turn to him or away from him. We find that Christ himself claims to possess unique knowledge of God and does not hesitate to tell others that his knowledge of the Father's love, will, and purpose is genuine and there is no higher knowledge of God. He also claimed to be able to bring people to God or to bring God to people. He must have surprised his followers on more than one occasion when he assured them that no one could come to the Father except through him or that no one had seen the Father but himself. One of the most amazing claims he made was to have the power to forgive sins. This claim and the exercise of it often produced tension between him and the religious leaders of the time. But he never wavered in this claim. The critics around him were in reality correct in holding to the idea that God alone can forgive sins. He went even further; he placed himself at the very center of the Kingdom of God and claimed to be the "way, the truth and the life." He claimed to be the center and the goal of history, and he spoke of his return as the most significant event of the future. Then, as we have seen, he claimed to be sinless. He could challenge his hearers to convict him of any sin.

(3) Our Experience Tests His Claims

His followers accepted the claims he made for himself and later they repeated them in their preaching and teaching about him. So far as we know, there is no example of his disciples who were with him to the end rejecting these claims. From that time until the present day there has been an ever growing circle of men and women who have accepted the claims Christ made for himself and in so doing have found strength, inspiration, and hope. It is possible even yet for each person to test these claims for himself We may ask, "Does Christ really bring

God to me?'' Is there anything unique about his person as seen in the gospels? Do I feel I have been forgiven when I confess my sins through him? Does he give richer meaning to my life? Do I have an easy conscience when I turn a deaf ear to his demands or call? To the Christian he is both Lord and Saviour. But each one of us has to find these things in Christ for himself. We must taste and see that he is Lord and that he is good. After all it is because of what happens in our own experience with him that his work of redemption becomes real and meaningful to us. Once we have stood at the foot of his cross and heard his words of forgiveness or in the stresses and strains of life have known the power of his resurrection, we can exclaim with Thomas, ''My Lord and my God!'' (John 20:28).

4. What Is Christ's Work as Redeemer?

(1) Christ Has a Three-fold Work

Christ has been called the "Mediator of the Covenant of Grace," in our Presbyterian thought, and in truth he is that—this is his work. Here again we may express our gratitude to John Calvin for bringing together the threads pertaining to the work of Christ as Redeemer in such a way as to give permanent expression to our conception of his redeeming work. It is summed up admirably in *The Shorter Catechism*: "Christ as our Redeemer, executeth the offices of a prophet, of a priest, and of a king, both in his estate of humiliation and exaltation" (Question 23). There are differences of opinion as to the value of this rather formal division of the work of Christ and it would be a mistake to try to force the redeeming work of Christ into any human mould of thought. It would be harmful, too, if we did not realize that we cannot isolate any one of these functions from the other; they are inseparably bound together. The Prophet, Priest, and King in the Old Testament were all anointed to fulfill their respective roles in Israel. These three phases of the religious life of the Old Testament give us the Hebraic ideal for the people of God whom he had redeemed out of Egypt. It shows what God was trying to do for his people through all these representatives. It thus serves to give us a high conception of the work of Christ for the people of God in the New Testament—those redeemed in Christ.

The main thrust of Christ's work as our Redeemer is to restore our broken relationship with God. Considering his work in the light of these three offices enables us to see what it takes to restore that relationship which is a highly personal one. We must be enlightened concerning God's will both toward and for him. The barriers we have erected between ourselves and God must be torn down. Then, there must come a new power, the principle of a new life with God which can come only through the lordship of Christ. God's redemptive love can become real in our lives only as we once more live in fellowship with him—Christ's work of redemption is designed to make this possible.

(2) His Work as Prophet

As prophet, Christ makes God's will known to us. Here we repeat again that man's great concern in religion is to know how God feels *toward* him. First, Christ assures us that God is love, gracious, forgiving and full of mercy. He is like the father in the story of the Prodigal Son, ever waiting for the return of his erring sons. But Christ, as prophet, also declares God's will *for* us in his own teachings. We cannot find God's will more perfectly set forth than in the words of Christ. The Sermon on the Mount, parables, and conversations serve to show God's will for us. Also, in the life of Christ we have the will of God set *before* us. We do not want to imitate Christ in any slavish, mechanical fashion but we do know as Christians that his way of living remains as unchallenged and unattained pattern for us. Finally, Christ as prophet also makes known God's will *in* us by the work of the Holy Spirit. He gives us the Holy Spirit who is in a real sense the "will of God in us" and that will has always been known to Christian faith as love. By way of summary, Christ is a prophet in that he makes known God's will *toward* us, *for* us, *before* us, and *in* us. Of course his work of a prophet is still going on. Wherever the gospel is preached, God's will *toward* us is declared, his will *for* us is taught, his will is set *before* us in the life of Christ and his will *in* us is begun by the Holy Spirit.

(3) His Work as Priest

We believe that Christ as Priest has broken down the barriers that sin placed between God and humanity. As seen above, his death on the cross reveals both the love and the justice of God. Christ is our spokesman, our representative before God. As the Word, he not only bridges the chasm between God and man from the divine, but also from the human side. He throws himself into the chasm by his death; he takes our place. His homely expression concerning himself as the "door of the sheepfold" gives us an idea of the meaning of his priestly work here. It is the picture of a shepherd who at night lies down across the door of the fold so that the sheep cannot be harmed in any way. Christ has taken our place that we may not have to bear the awful burden of our guilt. When Christ became our great High Priest he made every man a priest and in his continuing interest and concern in our redemption his priestly work goes on all the time.

In this work of Christ as our Priest we can see that God is expressing himself to us and for us in terms of grace and forgiveness. Christ makes known to us God's holy love as a reality; he makes God real to us. God in Christ's death reveals himself as nowhere else. Christ had to bring more than truth concerning God; although he did bring that, he had to embody that truth in his own life and thus make it real. Nothing is more real than that which comes through personal beings. He had to assume human form so as to present the reality of God's love in the clearest way. In this embodiment of love he could be everything God meant man to be when he created him. This was the only way man could be restored to God and to the high destiny God had intended for him from the beginning.

(4) His Work as King

Jesus came preaching the gospel of the Kingdom; he spent his ministry doing the work of the Kingdom—works of a redemptive nature—and he refused to engage in any other activities. In many of his sayings about the Kingdom he is seen to regard himself as the center and as the bearer of the redemptive work of the Kingdom. Hence the instinct that has led men to think of him as King has been quite sound. First, we may say that Christ holds sway over a universal Kingdom in that all things have been put under his feet. Perhaps it would not be incorrect to say God is ruling the world through Christ. He has always been regarded as ruling over the Church in a special way. The Church is the dominion of Christ. But as individuals Christ must exercise lordship in our hearts. As the Lord of all life, and the life of each one of us, he has complete sovereignty over us. We must give him control for he cannot undo the awful effects of sin in us unless we let him take over and we become his obedient servants. We must be willing to let him work in us and by the work of his spirit produce in us those qualities of life God intended us to have. If Christ is allowed to become King and Lord of life there need be no fear of anything in all the world. He truthfully defends us against all his and our enemies.

5. Under What Conditions Is Christ's Work as Redeemer Done?

The earthly life of our Lord has been spoken of as the "estate of humiliation," and has been described as consisting of five states. Christ came into this world in a very lowly fashion, lived a life subject to all the strains, stresses, hostilities, and threats of human existence. For our sakes he came under the yoke of the law and accepted its exacting demands for himself. He died the cruel and ignominious death of the cross, a fate he never deserved. He was buried in a borrowed tomb, that is, he came under the power of death. Finally, his descent into hell brought him to the lowest depths. It would be a sad and sorry story if that were the end. But it is not. On the first Easter morning his exaltation began. He rose from the dead. After forty days he ascended into heaven. He now sits on the right hand of God. In time he will return, and will judge all men. As there were five steps in his path downward, five may be seen on the road to glory, known as his "estate of exaltation." We note that his downward movement is like a road that drops over a hill and joins with the road leading up another hill. Truly for him the way of the Cross led to glory. "Therefore God has highly exalted him and bestowed on him the name which is above every name, that at the name of Jesus every knee should bow, in heaven and on earth and under the earth, and every tongue should confess that Jesus Christ is Lord, to the glory of God the Father" (Philippians 2:9–11).

Suggested Reading:

> *Call to Faith*, Chapters 5, 6.
> *Confession of Faith*, Chapter 8.
> *Shorter Catechism*, Questions 20–28.
> Scripture, Psalm 22; Isaiah 53; Matthew 16:13–28; Matthew 26:28; Luke 2:1–20; John 14, 15; Philemon 2:5–12; Colossians 1:12–20; Revelation 11:15.

7.

Our Presbyterian Belief About the CHURCH

Someone has said that the Church is the "strangest thing in the world." This is because it is impossible to kill it. Persecution may drive it under ground as when early Christians had to live in catacombs, often several stories under the surface of the earth. The truth seems to be that the Church always looks to the world around it as if it were about ready to die, yet it never does. Again, it often seems to be tottering near the brink because of corruption, error or materialism, but the Spirit of God begins his work of renewal and the "dead bones" begin to move and become alive once more. The fact is that with the exception of the family, the Church is probably the oldest continuing institution in our western society.

The Church is about ten times older than our nation, and it is several times older than the British Empire. A citizen of the Roman world of the first century of the Christian era would no doubt feel more at home in the Church today than anywhere else. This community we call the Church goes back much further than that, however, for it is rooted in history centuries before Christ. It claims the heritage of both Abraham and Moses and we feel that the Old Testament characters belong as much to us as the persons who are known to us in the New Testament.

1. Is the Church Really Important?

The Bible assures us that the Church is very important. We could sum up all the teachings of the Bible in two great doctrines—what it tells us about God and about the Church, his people. In Scripture we find that God is largely made known to us by his dealings with the Church. She derives her significance mostly from the fact that she is not something to which man gave existence in her earthly form. The Church gets her life from God whose almighty power and redemptive purpose are made known to us in Christ. God first gave life to the Church in the Old Testament when he called Abraham to go out into an unknown country. He began the Church anew in Christ who gathered a small band of men to be with him and to learn of him. It has been said that once Abraham was the whole Church of God. Then again, Christ was the whole Church of God. Christ alone carried the burden and promise of God's covenant with his people. He completely fulfilled the old covenant and he gave birth to the new one through his death and resurrection.

The Bible does not regard the Church as merely an organization or an institution as we often think of it. The Church is a community, a society, a people who sustain a peculiar relationship to God and to one another in Christ. The Church is a community of people whose hope is in the redeeming work of Jesus Christ. Her life is dependent upon the presence of the risen Lord, through the indwelling power of the Holy Spirit. This life that bursts forth in the Church cannot be put into words, but great words like faith, hope, and love are used to try to express it; but they are inadequate. The New Testament can speak of her only by using metaphors. These are helpful if not taken too literally. The Church is so important that many have no hesitation in saying that it was the Church, as God's people in Christ, God had in mind in the creation of the world.

2. How Is the Church Described?

Paul writes of the Church as "the mother of us all," and this is because she gives birth to the children of God. How did we come to know God as our Father? How did we come to know about the Word of God? Where did we learn about the strange new power that brings us the abundant life and makes us new persons in Christ? It may have been from our parents, our minister, or our church school teacher who first told us of the living Word of God. But some place along the line of our learning these things we will find that the Church has been at work. It has always been so, for without the Church we would not have known about God's redeeming love. Most of us know from experience what John Calvin meant when, in writing of the Church as mother, he said: "There is no other way of entrance into life, unless we are conceived by her, born of her, nourished at her breast, and continually preserved under her care and government."

The New Testament also calls the Church "the Body of Christ." Of course, this does not mean that the Church is an organism like a vegetable or an animal. To think of the Church in this light is to fail to grasp her true nature. The Church is called the "Body of Christ" because in many resspects it is like a human body. Thus the basic idea suggested by this metaphor is that the Church cannot exist independently of Christ. As he imparts his life to the Church she must also share in all Christ has experienced.

Although Christ is not now physically on earth, the Church lives in the world as Christ did; she bears his testimony, shares his sufferings, in a sense dies with him, lives with him and waits for him in hope. The Church throughout the world is the Body of Christ because she is the extension of his life and work into the life of the world today.

3. What Is the Old Testament Background of the Church?

The people of God in the Old Testament formed a visible community which can be traced with unbroken continuity through the centuries. We believe that it was preparatory to the Christian Church and that, in the fullness of time, it gave way to that society of God's people in Christ in the New Testament. We may gather from this that both the nature and the necessity of the Church are grounded in the fact and character of revelation.

That is, wherever the revelation of God is received and an appropriate response is made, there you will have the possibility of a people of God, or the Church. That is why it seems as foolish and absurd, from the point of view of the Bible, to ask whether a man can be a Christian without belonging to the Church as to ask whether a man can be a Jew without belonging to the Israel of God. There are some distinguishing marks of the Church that flow from her origin in the Old Testament, due to the fact that she is ultimately grounded on the revelation of God to man.

(1) The Church Sprang Out of Personal Relationship

The first important fact about the origin of the Church in the Old Testament is that she sprang out of God's personal relationship to men and women. The very term revelation implies three things: a revealer, that which is disclosed, and the recipient of the revelation. The first and last are both personal and the third, that which is given, is of concern to them as personal beings. We can say, therefore, that where there are persons who respond to divine revelation, that is to God's promise of grace, there you have the beginning of a people of God, or the Church. We believe that primarily God's relation to man is personal, whether we think of his activity as being that of Creation, Providence, or Redemption. Creation is what has been called "just God's bid for fellowship." Providence is carried on in relation to persons through prayer, the selection of men and women to carry out his will, and the basic moral nature of humans. Redemption is of course personal through and through, and Christ is the person by whom it comes to us.

Because the Church did come into being as a result of the personal relationship between personal beings—God and man—we can get a much deeper and clearer understanding of the secret of the meaning of personal existence itself. It means to us that relationship between personal beings gives us an insight into the essential nature of reality we find no where else. Throughout the entire Bible, sin destroys that fellowship. It separates a person from God and leaves him estranged from both his Maker and his neighbor. Salvation is the restoration of that fellowship, as we have seen, and it also brings a restoration of fellowship with others. This is why we can never lose sight of the Church as a fellowship of the forgiven and the forgiving; it is this in the New Testament.

(2) The Church Began as a Community

As we look at the origin of the Church in the Old Testament, we see at once that it is a community of persons called into fellowship with

God and with one another. The story of Israel is that of a community. We cannot understand the Old Testament apart from the conception of the solidarity of the nation. The "law of community" gives us the basis of the Hebrew conception of history. The covenants for the most part are made with the leaders as representatives of the people as a whole. This is true of the covenants made with Abraham, Isaac, and Jacob. Even the history of the people is recorded as though it were the story of an individual. Israel is thought of as a child in Hosea (11:1–4). Jeremiah, who first prophesied that the old covenant would give way to a new one, also said that the new covenant would be with the "house" of Israel.

Many things could be said about the value of this conception in the common life of Israel. It tempered the despotism of the monarchs of the nation. Even David could not break the spirit of community in his treatment of Uriah. Elijah strongly rebuked Ahab for permitting Jezebel to take the life of Naboth to get his vineyard. It also served to curb the greed of the wealthy and to provide security for the poor. It helped to check the tendency in Israel towards the worship of idols. The prophets like Jeremiah and Isaiah looked with scorn upon the absurd notion and practice that men and women with intelligence and personality should even think of falling down before images made of wood and stone and saying to them, "My Father." They saw the evil effects of idol worship on the character and persons of their fellow countrymen in the awful practice of human sacrifice and religious prostitution. They knew that people tend to become like that which they worship, and when they worship lifeless images they in time come to think of all of life in impersonal terms. The result is that "man's inhumanity to man will make countless millions mourn." The Church at Pentecost is born as a community.

(3) The Growth of the Idea of Individual Responsibility

The Church in the Old Testament was somewhat belatedly marked by the growing sense of individual responsibility. Ezekiel and Jeremiah both rejected the old slogan that if the fathers eat sour grapes the children's teeth will be set on edge. They said each of us must answer for his own sins. This principle of the Old Testament Church comes to focus most clearly in the prophetic consciousness of God. Once the prophet felt that God had given him a message he would declare it, come what may. Peter in Acts shows us that such a mind must obey God rather than men. Calvin closes his *Instruction in Faith* with Peter's words. A modern philosopher has said that one of the most difficult problems of our human existence is to adapt the growing selfhood of the individual into the life of the community. This issue brought disciplinary measures in the early Church; it often lies at the bottom of the difference in opinion concerning Church government. Paul declares that where the Spirit of the Lord is there is liberty—that is the way we get both responsibility and freedom. These two belong together. The former without freedom brings tyranny; freedom without responsibility breeds anarchy—the disease of modern culture. The freedom of the individual was assured at Pentecost, and achieved by the Apostle Paul.

(4) The Church Is to Be Universal

A fourth major characteristic of this Old Testament "people of God" was the divine intention that it become universal. This is obvious from the call of Abraham (Genesis 12:3; 17:5; 22:18). Peter's use of the prophecy of Joel concerning the coming of the Holy Spirit is to show that his coming is to usher in the era of a universal Christian community. We find the same emphasis in the great prophets of the Old Testament (Isaiah 2:1; Micah 4:1–5; Amos 8:22). Perhaps to quote one such passage will suffice: "In that day shall Israel be the third with Egypt and with Assyria, a blessing in the midst of the earth; for that Jehovah of hosts hath blessed them, saying, Blessed be Egypt my people, and Assyria the work of my hands, and Israel mine inheritance" (Isaiah 19:24,25). The religious thought of the time of our Lord in Israel had apparently lost sight of this note of universality that God intended for his people. The contemporaries of Jesus sensed that he was moving toward a breakdown of the narrow walls of Judaism. So much so that Joseph Klausner, a well known Jewish writer of today, says that the Jews put Christ to death because he was a Jew bent on the destruction of Jewry. As just noted the emphasis came back into the Church's teaching at Pentecost, but Peter was not yet ready for such a final stretch of his mind. It was only after the conversion of Saul that Christianity came into its own as a universal religion. He died to make the Church world-wide. To jump the centuries, we can say that John

Calvin was one of the most ecumenical minded men of his century and said that he hoped to see the Church planted everywhere in our world.

(5) The Church Was Born in Faith

The Church in the Old Testament also was the result of faith on the part of the people of God. We are told that Abraham believed God, and ever after he was spoken of as an outstanding example of faith. Paul frequently referred to him as the greatest instance of faith in the Old Testament. The eleventh chapter of the Epistle to the Hebrews gives us an idea of the way in which one New Testament writer regards the exercise of faith in the history of Israel. Of course, it remained for Paul to become the greatest champion of the doctrine of salvation by faith of all time, but it is well to remember that faith has been a characteristic of the Church from its beginning. It is the first response man makes to God's promise of grace. Justification by faith was a cardinal principle of the Protestant Reformation and both Luther and Calvin agreed that it was of the very essence of the true gospel.

4. How Can We Tell the True Church?

Where is the true Church? The shortest answer is to say that where Christ is, there is the Church, for without him there would be no Christian Church. As Protestants, we do not distinguish the true Church by some official pedigree, or purely external sign. The Reformers held that the Church is present wherever the Word of God is truly preached and heard, wherever the Sacraments are rightly administered and received, and wherever church discipline is wisely enforced. Now, what happens to the community where these three elements are present? The preaching of the Word of God issues in faith; the observance of the Sacraments produces fellowship; and the proper fruit of discipline is freedom. We shall look at each of these briefly.

The heart of the gospel is God's promise of redemption in Christ. When the grace of God promised in the gospel is accepted by faith we have the proper response of man to the preaching of God's Word. Faith is the sense of God's mercy in Christ and when we find it anywhere it means the gospel has been preached. But Christ is set forth for those who have faith even more vividly in the Sacraments. Christ is present in the Sacraments, and where he is we have fellowship. This fellowship is expressed in two significant acts, Baptism and the Lord's Supper. The third mark of the Church is discipline. The highest form of discipline is that inner, spiritual control which comes from the assurance that we should obey God rather than men. Paul called it freedom from the law. Luther saw it as being bound to God at the very center of existence and therefore, being bound by no external laws of any kind. One really gets this freedom only when his chief end in life is to live for the glory of God. In sum, *faith* is the response to a promise, *fellowship* is the response to a person, and *freedom* is response to a power. The Church, then, is the community of people who have *faith* in God's promise, the *fellowship* of those who have felt the presence of Christ in the Sacraments, a company of those who in *freedom* are empowered by the Holy Spirit to set themselves to do the will of God.

5. What Are the Purpose and Mission of the Church?

We come now to ask ourselves why do we have a Church in the world anyway? We may be able to answer this question in several different ways but the replies would really amount to the same thing. Our Confession of Faith speaks of the Church as the "body of the elect" and conceives her purpose as the "gathering of the People of God" in one great fellowship. Again, we may say that the Church exists to be a living testimony to the redeeming love of God in Christ and is the vehicle through which God's love is made known and His will done upon earth. The Church may be thought of as being here for the purpose of overcoming evil and enthroning good so that God's will may be done on earth as it is in heaven. Recently much stress has been given to the purpose of the Church as being that of increasing the love of God and neighbor. This is basic, for at the very foundation of all we think or say in Christian faith is the statement of our Lord, quoting from the Old Testament, that the sum of the Ten Commandments is to love God and our neighbor. These various expressions of the purpose of the Church can be summed up in the peculiar language of our Presbyterian faith by saying the Church on earth exists for the glory of God, for this is true regardless of the words used. And this means that the Church was given existence in order to disclose the love, purpose, and character of God—that is what it means to glorify him.

We conceive the mission of the Church more concretely in terms of her great task of evangelism, world missions, her educational work, and the nurturing of men and women in the Christian faith. Thus preaching the word of God in eveiy conceivable way and place, teaching men and women to become more intelligent and responsible Christians, and helping them to let their light so shine that God may be glorified—this and much more belong to the mission of the Church. The Church should offer men and women a place of worship, for as William Temple said, the most important thing we can do in a world like this is to worship and pray. The Church should offer hope and succour to those who have felt most severely the attacks of demonic forces of our time as Jesus was concerned to help those of his day who were most damaged by evil—sinners, publicans, harlots. The Church can and must be a critic, a sort of conscience in a world beset by all kinds of evil, and in which pagan influences seem to be growing in strength and popularity. It is no small part of the mission of the Church to display to the world the principle of the cross as she re-enacts this in her own life by ever living under the shadow of the cross. The Church stands in a world obsessed with notions of space and time, pointing men and women to the mystery of death and to the hope of life after death where our highest ideals for ourselves may become a reality.

After all the Church is but a foretaste of more wonderful things yet to come. Those in the Church are no more than pilgrims on earth. With staff in hand, they move along up the valleys and over the hills. Once in a great while the clouds lift and they can see but for a moment the heights beyond. They sing the songs of Zion as they go. In their deeper moments of patient suffering and quiet waiting they hear the echoes of a grander music. Yet the glories of the Kingdom in its fullness are not for their "earth-stuck" eyes. But they go on in hope. Their God has said: "Thou shalt be my people and I will be thy God forever."

Suggested Reading:

Introduction to the Reformed Tradition, Chapter V.
Call to Faith, Chapters 8, 9.
Confession of Faith, Chapters 27, 28.
Shorter Catechism, Questions 102, 103.
Scripture, Genesis 17:1–9; Exodus 19; Jeremiah 31:31–34; Matthew 17:13–19; Acts 2:1–47; Ephesians 1, 2; Revelation 21:1–7.

8.

Our Presbyterian Belief
About the SACRAMENTS
(or Signs)

Perhaps one of the oldest definitions of a Sacrament is the one that has come to us from Augustine. He said it "is a visible sign or form of invisible grace." Calvin also gives a very good definition of a Sacrament as "a testimony of God's favor toward us, confirmed by an outward sign, with a mutual testifying of our godliness toward him." To put the meaning of the term Sacrament more in the language of our time we could say it is a physical act that signifies a spiritual relationship between personal beings.

From time immemorial the Sacraments have held a high place in both Christian thought and worship. The observance of the Lord's Supper has always been regarded as the highest point in worship. In Geneva, Calvin believed it should be administered every Sunday and would have done so had he not met with opposition from members of the Church. They finally agreed to celebrate Holy Communion once a month. This historical incident should give us some idea of the importance ascribed to the place of the Lord's Supper in our Presbyterian thought and piety.

1. What Is the Purpose of the Sacraments?

(1) They Do Not Bring Extra Grace

Our Presbyterian conception of the Sacraments is that they enable us to apprehend more clearly and more vividly the presence of Christ than we are able to do from merely hearing or reading the Word of God. They are in reality the word of God in a visible form as a means of more indelibly stamping upon our minds and hearts the great realities of the gospel. The Sacraments are a dramatic presentation of the great promises of God to man in Christ. They are the Word in action, in a more lively fashion than when merely written.

It is our conviction that the Sacraments do not add any distinct value or benefit to the redemptive work of Christ as it is set forth in the Bible. We believe that Christ, the living Word, is set forth in Scripture and in the oral preaching of the gospel. We are certain he is so fully and adequately given us in the gospel that nothing else, not even a Sacrament, can add to the grace which comes to us when we accept him through faith. The Sacraments do serve, however, to make more vivid, to portray more dramatically, and to set forth visibly Christ as the bearer of our redemption. Perhaps an illustration will help to clarify what we are trying to say here about the Sacraments. We may hear over the radio a familiar voice like that of our President speaking an important message. If we were to turn from the radio to the television we would hear the same voice, but in addition to that we would see his image, note the expression on his face, the movements of his body, his frowns and his smiles. We learn nothing new as to the truth he speaks. Now the Sacraments are to the preaching of the gospel what television is to radio.

(2) They Enable Faith to Grow

What we have been saying about a Sacrament thus far gives us a cue to the real purpose of these visible signs used in Christian worship. There is always a personal relationship between God and the believer in the participation of either of the Sacraments of our Church. We may put it something like this: the Sacraments simply point to the promise of God's grace in the gospel. They say to us, by this simple act or rite we can be assured that God loves us, he cares for us, he has infinite concern for our welfare. It is true these signs set before us are more physical objects but they speak to us concerning the profoundest truths and realities there are—they are saying to us that just as sure as we behold these physical objects there lie behind them spiritual realities which God wants us to have.

(3) The Holy Spirit Is at Work

You may be asking yourself by this time, "How does all of this we are talking about produce faith?" Of course, faith comes to us as a gift of the Holy Spirit. But this should not be taken to mean this gift is thrust upon us in a coercive fashion and from beyond us. It means that just as the Holy Spirit makes the promise of the gospel a real and personal thing to us he also presents this visible evidence of God's grace as set forth in the Sacraments to us in the same way. In other words, the creative power of the Holy Spirit is at work in our hearts as we see what God has done for us as portrayed in the Sacraments. We realize the grace of God works faith in our heart as we see him in action in our behalf, for God is as active in the administration of the Sacraments as any person who participates in them. He gives us faith in him by showing us what he has done, is doing and will do for us in Christ. Our doubt, mistrust are overcome when we fully realize God means what he says in putting before our very eyes these symbols of his love and grace.

(4) The Sacraments Make Christ Real

Another way of expressing the purpose of the Sacraments is to say they make Christ more real to us. In calling them "signs" Christian thought has stressed the fact that we must never let the glance of faith end with these visible things alone. They also serve the purpose of declaring the reality of the age to come as well as giving us a foretaste of what is in store for us in the future. The Church is in a sense deeply rooted in our world of time and space but it ever clings to the invisible spiritual reality of the Kingdom of God. The Sacraments sharpen and deepen our faith in the reality of that unseen world and assure us that man lives in more than one dimension—he not only lives in that invisible realm now but it is to be his real and only home in time to come.

2. When Do We Have a Sacrament?

(1) The Sacraments and the Word

The elements of water in Baptism and of bread and wine in Communion do not of themselves constitute a Sacrament when prepared and brought together at the table. It is necessary to relate these elements to the redemptive work of Christ as it is given in Scripture. Traditionally, therefore, we have sought to relate God's promise of grace in the Bible to the portrayal of it in the Sacraments by reading from the Bible what is usually called "the words of institution." Our common practice in this respect has been far more consistent as regards the Lord's Supper than it has been with reference to Baptism. It is not entirely clear that we are given these words of institution for Baptism in the same way we are those pertaining to Communion. In the great commission Jesus' followers were told to make disciples of all nations "baptizing them in the name of the Father and of the Son and of the Holy Spirit" (Matthew 28:19).

In the Upper Room, on the night of betrayal, Jesus established the Sacrament of the Lord's Supper. In the gospel accounts of this scene, as well as in the description of it given us by Paul in the eleventh chapter of First Corinthians, Christ told his disciples the bread they were to eat and the wine they were to drink represented his body and blood. The words he used in setting forth his sacrificial death in this first Supper, from any of the records found in Scripture, may be regarded as valid for the institution of this Sacrament. If, however, we were to perform outwardly either of these rites without any mention of, or reference to, their meaning as contained in Scripture we do not have a Sacrament. We may readily see the reason why our Presbyterian Church has so stubbornly adhered to this position is because of the deep conviction that either one of these signs must be inseparably related to the redemptive work of Christ as found in Scripture.

(2) The Holy Spirit and Faith Are Needed

From the point of view of those of us who partake of the Sacraments, even after the elements used have been properly related to the Word of God and set aside by prayer on the part of the minister, two other things are necessary if we are to derive the spiritual benefits declared in them. It is just as necessary for us to have the presence of the

Holy Spirit in our hearts as we sit around the Communion Table as it is to have his power working in us when we are listening to or reading the Bible itself. That is to say, the Holy Spirit must be present to make real and personal to us the grace signified in the Sacrament. Otherwise our eating of the bread and drinking of the wine would have no more spiritual significance than an ordinary meal. The other element necessary to a genuine participation in the Sacraments is faith. As the Holy Spirit creates faith in us we are able to apprehend more clearly and fully the marvelous grace of God and his inexhaustible mercies in Christ to which the Sacraments point. The living Christ becomes present only to a living faith. Again, without the work of faith we do not feed upon the body and blood of our Lord.

3. How Have Christian Views of the Sacrament Differed?

(1) Differences About Baptism

One of the ironical things in Church history is that the Sacraments which symbolize unity and fellowship have often become the means of dividing Christians. This is true of both Baptism and of the Lord's Supper, although differences concerning the latter have been sharper and have brought greater divisions. As to Baptism, there are those who believe it has a saving power and brings us redemption. For instance, this is the teaching of the Roman Catholic Church as well as some branches of Protestantism. The Church has been divided also by differences of opinion concerning the mode of Baptism—whether it should be administered by sprinkling, pouring, or immersion. Presbyterians have almost without exception adhered to sprinkling or pouring while maintaining that actually the form is a matter of little importance. Most Baptists practice immersion exclusively. One of the difficult things about this controversy is that it is not easy to settle it by an appeal to the New Testament. We believe, however, that sprinkling is scriptural and that it is the most suitable mode of Baptism.

(2) Zwingli's View of Communion

The sharpest differences between Christians have reference to the meaning of the Lord's Supper. Four different views concerning the way in which Christ is present in the Eucharist have come down to us from the Protestant Reformation of the sixteenth century. Zwingli, the Swiss reformer, plunged into a bitter argument with Martin Luther on this question. This great Swiss leader believed that man's salvation comes through a direct relationship to God and grace is given directly by the Holy Spirit. For him, therefore, the Lord's Supper becomes largely a memorial calling to mind the death and resurrection of Christ. It is not easy to say exactly how the presence of Christ in the Supper was conceived by Zwingli. He apparently held that Christ is vividly present to memory somewhat as we are able to recall in a very lively sense some scene of early childhood. Certainly this view has merit so far as it goes and we shall not forget that our Lord said "do this in remembrance of me."

(3) The Lutheran View

Luther differed widely and with some bitterness from Zwingli. He interpreted the words "this is my body" in a literal sense and took them to mean that Jesus is physically present *in*, *with*, and *under* the elements of bread and wine. He believed strongly the believer does receive the actual substance of the Lord's body and blood as he places the elements in his mouth. He said when a person chews the bread he is chewing the Lord's body as though he were chewing a gristle between his teeth. The technical name for this view is consubstantiation, which literally means "with the substance." In order to maintain this sort of presence of Christ in the Sacrament, Luther was driven to the position that the glorified body of our Lord is now capable of being everywhere.

(4) The Teaching of Roman Catholicism

It is even more difficult for Presbyterians to follow the Roman Catholic view of Holy Communion or the Mass. In this interpretation there is a real change in the elements of bread and wine from mere natural objects to the actual body and blood of Christ. The substance of bread becomes that of Christ's body, and the substance of wine becomes his blood. This change that takes place is miraculous and occurs when the priest officiating utters the words of consecration. When the believer puts in his mouth the substance which looks like bread he is feeding on the real body of Christ. The same is true of the cup. The priest has the power to turn common bread and wine into the body and blood of our Lord. Consequently, there grew up the practice of withholding the communion entirely from children for fear of their dropping our Lord's body or spilling His blood. Later, only the priest was allowed to drink from the cup for fear of spilling its precious content. Thus, what we see at Communion still looks like bread and wine, smells like bread and wine and tastes like bread and wine, but what we eat and drink is the Lord's body and blood. This view of the Sacrament has been called transubstantiation which means a "crossing over of substance" from one kind to another. Roman Catholics also hold that Christ is offered in the Mass as a bloodless sacrifice over and over again, whereas Protestants believe Christ was offered but once as a sacrifice for the sins of the world.

(5) The Presbyterian View

John Calvin utterly rejected the Catholic notion of the Mass. He was as eager to secure the presence of Christ in this Sacrament as any of his contemporaries but he would not concede that Christ was present in the elements themselves. He tried, therefore, to present a view which would more or less mediate between the views of Zwingli and Luther. He said we do not receive the presence of Christ because the elements have been turned into His body and blood, nor because his body and blood are present *in*, *with*, and *under* them, but he is present to the believer by faith through the secret power and work of the Holy Spirit. The sum and substance of Calvin's view has become a part of our Presbyterian belief although there have been variations in expressing it. *The Shorter Catechism* says that believers are "not after a corporal and carnal manner, but by faith, made partakers of his body and blood, with all his benefits, to their spiritual nourishment and growth in grace" (Question 96).

(6) All Agree in Seeking the Presence of Christ

In spite of the differences we have noticed in the above views, there is a common effort to believe Christ is somehow present in the Lord's Supper. If this were not true we would be led to discard this Sacrament altogether, as the Quakers have done. One difficulty in our time is that the Sacraments have lost much of their basic meaning even to Christians. For many, the peculiar practice of Baptism and the administering of the Lord's Supper seem like so much foolishness. Perhaps our need is to recapture that faith which enabled our forefathers vividly to see the realities the Sacraments set forth and keenly to feel the presence of the living Lord. Sacraments in the Church have from the beginning been related to experiences charged with profound meaning. It is no wonder then, that if such experiences are no longer meaningful to men and women they regard the participation and the Sacraments as little short of empty skulduggery. It is not enough to go on clinging to them for the only reason that we can say Christ established them. He did many things we no longer do. We shall have once more to recover in our own experience those realities to which the Sacraments point.

4. What Does Baptism Say to Us?

(1) Baptism Means a New Life

Baptism speaks to us of the death and resurrection of Christ, for had he not died and risen it would be without meaning. This is the significance of those passages of Scripture that speak of our being buried with Christ in Baptism. What they are saying is that this initial act performed for a Christian, when he enters the Church, indicates he has made a new beginning and has left the old way of life behind. He is dead to the world and alive unto Christ. They mean he is now stepping over into the realm, the Church, whose life is a gift of the Spirit who will make manifest in him the power of the resurrection.

(2) It Means We Are Forgiven

Baptism also signifies a cleansing from sin, the forgiveness of all our past sins, and says to us we may now become free from the power and corruption of sin. It also symbolizes the coming of the Holy Spirit into our life who will enable us "more and more to die unto sin and to live unto righteousness." These are not separate realities; they are simply several aspects of the same reality. They tell us of a new life, a new start, a cleansing and a possibility of renewal.

(3) It Means We Are in the Church

Baptism is a sign or a mark of our initiation into the Church, of our stepping over the threshold into a new community and a new dimension of life. It is the stamp or the mark which every individual receives as he enters into the community of the people of God in Christ. Let us ask, then, to whom is Baptism to be administered? All adults who have not been baptized in infancy receive this rite upon entrance into the Church. The branches of the Christian Church that stress community also administer Baptism to children of Christian parents. Our Presbyterian doctrine of the covenant holds we are justified in baptizing children because of the faith of the parents, although the child himself does not yet have the faith. Such a child is really born a member of the covenant society, that is the hand of God has placed him in that community in which redemption is taking place. We believe God has promised to be to that child what he is to his parents. Because Baptism does mark the initial step into the Church it is administered but once.

5. What Is the Meaning of the Lord's Supper?

We have already dealt with the various views of the Lord's Supper. We have now to look more closely into the meaning in experience and to faith of this time-honored form of worship. We can find several elements in this Sacrament which give it meaning. It is observed as a perpetual memory of the death of Christ for our sins. It is an unchanging pledge of his undying love. He said, "this do in remembrance of me." This experience can become real to us in Communion if we search our memory to rediscover all that Christ has meant to us. We may ask ourselves such questions as, when did I first hear the name of Jesus? What meaning did it have for me? When did his name take on meaning in my experience? What has he meant in life to me?

The Lord's Supper is also a bond of our union with Christ and with each other as members of his mystical body, the Church. The Holy Spirit brings each of us to Christ, but the same Spirit binds us to each other in Christian fellowship. Again, his promise is sealed to us in the Sacrament and we may rest assured it will never fail. Our response to this is a renewal of our obedience to him and a sincere expression of our resolute purpose ever to be true to him. As we have already seen, we have in this rite the blessed assurance of Christ's name. We are also filled with a sense of joy as we remember what God has done for us in Christ. Communion should be a time of thanksgiving; that is the meaning of the word Eucharist. But it is also a moment of hope for it speaks to us of his coming again. "For now we see in a mirror dimly, but then face to face." (1 Corinthians 13:12)

Suggested Reading:

> *Introduction to the Reformed Tradition*, Chapter V.
> *Call to Faith*, Chapter 12.
> *Confession of Faith*, Chapters 29–31.
> *Shorter Catechism*, Questions 91–97.
> Scripture, Matthew 3:13–17; 26:26–30; 28:19–20; Mark 14:22–26; Luke 22:14–20; 1 Corinthians 11:23–34.

9.

Our Presbyterian Belief About the Christian LIFE

The notion has often been expressed that it doesn't make any difference what we believe and it is the way we live that really matters. Nothing could be further from the truth than this, for the way we live stems from our belief. There is in reality a very close relation between belief and behavior. Our deepest convictions will ultimately express themselves in our attitudes, our relationships, and our actions. For instance, if one does not believe in life after death, everything done in life will be isolated from the vast realm of eternal values. The early Christian conviction concerning eternal life was so strong, and its values were so real, that men and women shaped their lives on earth according to those values rather than in accord with the standards of this world.

An equally great fallacy has existed to the effect that Christian thought or doctrine is not related to life; this also is false. Every major Christian doctrine may be seen to have some concrete relation to human experience. This is why the great so-called doctrinal portions of the letters of Paul in the New Testament, which set forth the truths of redemption, are usually followed by a fervent appeal to give them expression in daily life.

1. What Kind of Religious Experience Flows from Our Presbyterian Belief?

It is always interesting to observe that almost every major branch of the Christian Church will eventually produce its own type of religious experience, or piety, to use an old but very good term. Perhaps it is easier for us to detect the differences in piety of a Church like the Roman Catholic, as over against the pattern of experience in the Presbyterian Church than would be true if we would contrast ours with that of other Protestants. For instance, it is exceedingly difficult for us to understand the exalted position of the Virgin Mary in the Roman Church, the submission of lay members to the clergy, and even the often noticed regularity in attendance at Mass. Most of these elements in the practice of Roman Catholics grow out of particular doctrines of that Church.

In a similar fashion Calvinism has been influential in developing both a particular kind of devotional attitude as well as its own conception of the expression of the ethical teachings of Christianity. Let us consider some of the aspects of this unique pattern of Christian experience.

(1) We Are Dependent on God

We can begin by recalling the emphasis Presbyterians have always placed upon the sovereignty of God. This conception of God has produced a peculiar type of piety marked by a sense of complete dependence upon him. The consciousness of the absolute dependence on God can and has become a way of life. We not only recognize God as the giver of our physical life but also as the only source of our spiritual life. This notion is at the root of the doctrine of election and predestination. This way of life was very real and meaningful to early Calvinists and still has meaning for those who have vitally entered into it. It must be admitted, however, the modern mind has felt ill at ease at the thought of having to depend upon God for all things. In this attitude there is the failure to realize that it was this very sense of dependence upon divine power that made Calvinism such a dynamic force in western society.

(2) We Acknowledge the Majesty of God

Closely related to the sense of dependence upon God has been the feeling of awe before his eternal majesty. God is seen as one whose holiness sets him apart and above every thing he has created. In his presence man has a feeling of his own littleness as well as his own unworthiness. This view of God has created a feeling of reverence for him. When we come unto his presence in worship what we have to say to him or about him is not so important. We are there to listen to him speak to us for we know that it is indeed he who holds our destiny in the hollow of His hand. It also means when we are at worship our chief purpose is to adore, praise, exalt, and glorify him. This accounts for the objective nature of worship in the Presbyterian tradition. Our hymns are words of praise rather than expressions of subjective feelings. That is, our hymns are an attempt to acknowledge the majesty of God rather than to express how good we feel in his presence. From this point of view, the great hymn, "Our God, Our Help in Ages Past," is the expression of a more profound experience than such a song as "That Will Be Glory for Me."

(3) We Are Servants of God

Following close upon those two features of Christian experience our Presbyterian belief has also taught us that our highest aim in life is to live according to the will of God or to live in obedience to his will. The Christian is the obedient servant of his Lord. It is his responsibility to try to know the will of God and it is his duty to do it. He is conscious that he is to live in the light of God's will every moment of his life, in every decision he makes and in every course he pursues. Thus man is able to live for the glory of God in any calling God has placed him. A true picture of a Christian is that of a faithful, loyal, active, and obedient servant. It is that of a man receiving the grace of God in one hand, with the other stretched out in service. With one hand he grasps and with the other he grinds. To him the Church is not only concerned with the salvation of the individual but it should endeavor to make God's will known throughout society.

We may well image that Martin Luther and John Calvin found the same realities as they knelt before the cross of Christ. Both knew what it was to experience the saving grace of God through the cross. This glorious experience thrilled the soul of Luther to his very depths. He knew an inexpressible joy and yet he was ever trying to express it. We can almost imagine him clapping his hands and shouting, "Glory Alleluia!" Calvin may be thought of as kneeling beside him. He also has known what it means to be forgiven in Christ. He seems to be listening and looking upward, his whole body seems to be in stress and strain. If we were to ask him what he was doing, he would answer us by saying, "I am listening for a voice. I want to know what it says." Then suddenly his countenance becomes relaxed and he rises rapidly to his feet and goes out. Where is he going?—he is going out to spend and be spent, to burn the candle of his life down to the bottom for his Master.

(4) We Love God Through Love to Neighbor

This early piety of Presbyterians is also expressed in a charitable attitude toward others. The only way in which we can give visible, tangible, and concrete expression to our love for God is by loving our neighbor. It was also believed that every man in need is our neighbor, for he is made in the image of God. Also it was a basic conviction that God's will toward us is best expressed in terms of love in Christ, and God's will for us is best expressed by us in terms of love for our neighbor. If we put alongside these basic convictions a corollary teaching, common to the reformers of the sixteenth century, that everything we possess belongs to God, we can understand further the desire to practice generosity in daily life. All of these great leaders, including John Calvin, believed that we should put our belongings at the disposal of the Christian community when needed for the welfare of humanity or for the advancement of the Kingdom. This has been called the "Evangelical Principle of Possessions." Philip Melanchthon said Christians have all things in common and they should ever be willing to share with those in need. What he called "evangelical poverty" was the principle according to which we regard ourselves as merely the keepers of the property of another in relation to everything we possess. Of course this action was voluntary and was not in opposition to private ownership. It was a serious attempt to show the gratitude of the Christian for God's grace to him by his generosity to others. As a result of this tender piety a daily prayer of an early Calvinist contained words like these "Our

Lord, so bless the labor of my hands this day that when night comes I may have something to give to those in need."

(5) Prayer Is the Vital Breath of the Christian

The conception of God and the sense of dependence upon him have also given to our Presbyterian piety a strong conviction concerning the significance of prayer. It was Calvin's belief that prayer is the chief exercise of the Christian. In his book on theology he devotes considerable space to the meaning, the significance, and the manner of prayer. For him prayer was not our running to God with all our whims and fancies, only when we needed or wanted him. Prayer is a kind of atmosphere in which we live and move. It is a permanent, conscious, intimate, personal relationship which we sustain to God. Prayer is the expression of our deepest needs, desires, and highest aspirations. It is a rendering of our thanks unto God for His countless blessings and a constant seeking of his forgiving grace. When we pray we should endeavor so to open our lives to the influence of the power of the Spirit that he moves us to pray in accordance with the will of God.

2. What Has Been the Influence of Presbyterianism on Christian Living?

We often think that following the Reformation John Calvin's greatest influence was in the realm of doctrine. It is true his general system of theological thought spread throughout northern Europe, the British Isles, and the United States. We often forget, however, that the ethical system of early Presbyterianism, stemming from Calvin, had an even greater influence. There were those who accepted Calvin's moral teachings who were unable to follow him in doctrine. Georgia Harkness has said, for instance, that early Methodism followed his ethical system practically all the way. This has been true in many other Protestant areas.

(1) The Early Presbyterian Virtues

When we come to look at the main virtues of our early Presbyterian faith we are really surprised at their simplicity. They were such virtues as honesty, frugality, charity, sobriety, chastity, and industry. Each of these speaks for itself and, of course, all of them have gone into the making of our present western culture. Historians have spoken of these principles of living as middle class virtues. There is an element of truth in this description but it should not be pushed too far. In the first place we could say that all of these virtues are mentioned in the New Testament and most certainly the early Christians were not middle class. In the next place it should be observed that most of these virtues would belong to the personality of a Christian in any age or clime.

(2) The Development of These Virtues

We may follow this subject still further. It has been generally recognized that Martin Luther appealed largely to the upper class and nobility in Germany. There were in Germany at that time religious movements which spread largely among the masses of the people. The so-called lower class was not effectively brought into the Lutheran movement. In this era, however, there was an increasing middle class of people coming to the forefront. It was called the "third estate." This class had sprung up as a result of the rise of the merchant class of people and the growth of independent cities. Those who belonged to it had to struggle to establish their status in the social order of that day. Many of them had lost contact with the Roman Catholic Church because it frowned upon their preoccupation with making money and merchandising. Now it has been usually thought that Calvinism or early Presbyterianism made its appeal to this social group. And, of course, it is not a mere coincidence that the virtues Calvin set forth were the very ones that would apply to this class struggling for recognition. There is, however, another way in which we may look at this situation.

(3) These Virtues at Work

A British historian has said that early Calvinism made a strong appeal to the poor people of Europe. But once they embraced Calvinism and began to practice the simple virtues given above they would become more secure financially and would also eventually rise in the social order. In short, they would move toward becoming middle class. Wesley recognized the possibilities in this situation among his followers. He said there had to be a religious awakening about every third generation. This is the reason: Those who were at the bottom of the ladder, or the poor in spirit, have no way to look except up. When they become Christians they begin to practice these virtues we have designated. Their simple habits of life strengthen their financial situation but their religious zeal is in no way weakened by prosperity. But the second generation is likely to have less religious zeal but more concern about worldly goods. By the time the third generation comes along, the religious interest has pretty well died off and the pursuit of material things dominates. Thus a new religious awakening is necessary.

3. Can We Recapture the New Testament Way of Life?

It is fairly obvious to all of us that the virtues we have been describing do not exhaust the ideal for a Christian set forth in the New Testament. It may also be true that due to the changes that have come in our society we need to reconsider our all too conventional approach to the basic principles of Christian living. We need to take a good look at what our civilization is doing to the personalities of men and women of our time and go back to the New Testament once more to understand the secret of joyous, buoyant, triumphant Christian living in a world that seems ever to be on the brink of disaster. In this connection we could all profit greatly from the book *New Testament Christianity*, by J. B. Phillips. We may find that, after all, creative living is less determined by a detailed setting forth of certain things we should or should not do.

We can never get away from the basic moral principles laid down in the Ten Commandments. We can never forget the picture of a Christian Jesus gives us in the Beatitudes. We will want to study the pattern of life set before us in the remainder of the Sermon on the Mount. Often we will turn to Paul's description of the fruits of the Spirit in the twenty-second and twenty-third verses of the fifth chapter of Galatians. We should ever keep before us his description of the Christian life in First Corinthians (1 Corinthians 13). It has been said that when Paul wrote this chapter he kept thinking about Jesus. When we ponder it seriously in our twentieth century we are brought back to the fact already stressed, namely, that it is in the realm of personal relationships that we come closest to reality. Our Christian faith has repeatedly summed up the Christian life in terms of three great virtues—faith, hope, and love. We shall take a brief glance at each of these.

(1) Faith Is Basic

Anything that is to be said about Christian living must be fitted into the thought of eternal life. Faith, hope, and love all point to something beyong this world. We may look at it this way; faith is believing that we have here and now a small portion of the reality that is to come to us in eternity. That is, we believe we now have in Christ that quality of life in a small measure which we call eternal life. The Easter message not only says that Christ assures us of life after death but also that the life that is to be is ours now. This is the meaning of the New Testament usage of such a word as earnest or pledge concerning the Holy Spirit. The Holy Spirit is always pointing us to the life to come, but his presence in our life now means that the life which is to come is in a real sense ours now.

(2) Hope Is Constant

Hope is equally related to eternal life in Christian thought. It is a basic Christian teaching that without the hope of eternal life the things of this world are empty and meaningless. Thus our hope for good in this life has a sound basis only if there is another life to follow. Hope, therefore, is the Christian grace which leads us ever to believe that the present realities we now have in faith in a sort of "capsule" form will be ours in all fullness in that Kingdom without end.

(3) Love Is Lasting

Love is simply acting according to our faith and hope. If that eternal life is brought to us here and now according to faith, and if that quality of life faith now brings us is to be bestowed upon us in the fullest possible measure in the life to come, there is nothing left for the Christian but to live here and now in this world of space and time as he hopes to live in the eternal Kingdom. At this point we should remind ourselves of the words of Paul "So faith, hope, love abide, these three; but the greatest of these is love" (1 Corinthians 13:13). So the only thing we can live by in eternity is love; that's all there is left.

This thought can be made clearer by turning to a statement taken from Paul's letter to the Philippians. He says "but our commonwealth is in heaven" (3:20). James Moffatt's rendering of this passage gives exactly the sense which we have had in mind concerning eternal life. In his translation of the New Testament it reads like this, "we are a colony of heaven." Paul is saying to the Christians to whom he is writing, God has placed us as a colony in the world. But we really belong in the Kingdom of heaven; that is our real country. We are put here for the purpose of giving concrete expression to the values, way of life, and truths which belong to our true homeland. This imagery is derived from the common practice of the Roman Empire that sent retired military men and their families to various parts of the country to establish communities which would help to spread the Roman culture, embodying its traditions, customs, and way of life. It would be somewhat like a group of Americans, at the request of the President, going to Russia and settling there with the view of letting the people around them see what the highest principles of American democracy are like as they are expressed in community life.

The Church exists on earth as a kind of "sample" of the way of life of the eternal Kingdom of God. The Christian living here in this life, then, has such faith in the reality of the world to come, such hope that it will come in fullness and in glory that he endeavors to bring over into his life on earth the basic principles and values of the realm of eternal life and to give them concrete expression in his love both for God and for his neighbor. Here, once more, we touch upon the purpose of the Church which is to increase love to God and neighbor. This is so important in our earthly life because the love of God and each other is of the very essence of the life to come.

Suggested Reading:

Introduction to the Reformed Tradition, Chapter III.
Call to Faith, Chapters 9–13.
Confession of Faith, Chapters 15, 18–23.
Shorter Catechism, Questions 34–83.
Scripture, Exodus 20:1–17; Psalms 42, 73; Matthew 5:1–16; Luke 10:25–37; Romans 12; 1 Corinthians 13; Galatians 5:22, 23; Hebrews 11

10.

Our Presbyterian Belief About LAST THINGS (The End)

More than once it has been pointed out in our discussion of various aspects of our Christian faith that the gospel contains a message of eternal life here and now. It is quite possible, and it has happened more than once, that men get so concerned with life after death, and regard it so intently as the only part of human experience worth emphasizing, that the eternal qualities of this life in Christ are lost sight of or considerably diminished in thought. There is, however, an opposite error that often creeps out in the Church that is equally unbalanced and can lead to a crippling of the work and life of the Christian Church. It is the view that so stresses the presence of Christ in our earthly experience, and the power of the new life through our risen and living Lord that it tends to neglect, ignore, or sometimes deny the significance of the doctrine of the ultimate disclosure of our Saviour's glory in his return to judgment. The first extreme may even take a pessimistic view of this life and concentrate almost entirely on the return of our Lord and the events that are regarded as an essential part of his coming again. This interpretation may end up in apocalyptic daydreaming and wishful thinking about the future.

The second tendency may neglect the idea of the return of our Lord and may emphasize that here and now there come to us all the realities of Christian experience to be expected and all of the blessings of redemption we shall ever know are fully realized in history. According to this view, there will be no great portrayal of the presence of Christ at some future time; we can thus rest content with the realized presence through the Holy Spirit now. Some think of a final ending to events of history and the ushering in of eternity, or of the ultimate consummation of all things in the Kingdom without end. But they do not expect some specific disclosure of divine character such as we have in the Incarnation of our Lord. The objections to this outlook are fairly obvious. It is forced to ignore many passages of Scripture, in both the gospels and the epistles, and to direct attention almost exclusively to the Gospel of John in which the presence of Christ in this life is stressed. It also takes from the content of faith the dynamic element of future expectancy which marked the religion of the Old Testament, and became an essential part of the point of view of early Christians. Finally, one-sided stress upon the presence of Christ in this life may lead to the identification of our human plans and programs with the Kingdom of God and may eventually result in a thinning down of the spiritual values or even in a coming to terms with the secular world.

1. What Is the Christian View of Last Things?

(1) Christ Is the Center of the Future

Because of the possibility of differences of opinion as regards the meaning of the teaching of Scripture on "last things" we will do well to consider this question further. First, we can say that no view of the future of the world or of the individual that is not vitally related to Christ can be regarded as distinctively Christian. The belief in immortality, even in a resurrection of the dead, punishment after death, or a last judgment has been known to exist outside the Christian faith. The distinctive element about the future for Christian faith is that there will come a time when once more God will make a dramatic disclosure of himself in Christ, of his love and grace in the same person who so wonderfully showed us the Father in the long ago. That is, it is the coming of Jesus Christ that stands at the center of our Christian hope for the future. As God once came to us, and moved toward our world, he will again in the return of Christ reveal that same love. Christ will once again lead that divine movement of love toward the world and the individuals in it. The early Christians knew that Jesus would be their judge and they really had no qualms about the judgment. For them the coming again of Christ was as much an expression of God's love as when he came as a lowly babe in a manger in Bethlehem. And they thought that because he had so come he would most certainly return to the historical scene but this time in glory and majesty, yet still in love. As Calvin thought, the Christian need not fear the judgment, for the same Lord that died for him would be his judge—that meant that love, mercy, and grace would prevail.

(2) Election Brings Eternal Life

The early Christian conception of last things enables us to understand somewhat more clearly two doctrines which have often given students of our Presbyterian belief some difficulty. The first one is the doctrine of Election. Calvin taught it for at least three good reasons. First, he was certain that it was found in the Bible. Second, he knew from his own experience that he had done nothing toward his salvation other than to accept what the grace of God bestowed on him. Third, there was no way to explain the fact that when people hear the gospel proclaimed some stop, look, listen, and follow; others go on ignoring the gospel call. Those who turn around and follow Christ are no better, no more deserving or worthy than the rest. This mystery he could not explain except by saying that it must have been due to divine action. The Christian believes, then, that God loved him into existence as a spiritual person and this love creates in him that quality of life which will never perish. Election means that God sought me and found me and gave me his love freely. But it also means that he at the same time gave me a new kind of inner experience that springs forth unto life eternal. Hence every moment of life is filled with the meaning that shall never fade out. That is, inevitably if I have faith I get the "future look" that stretches out to eternity.

(3) God's Love Is Unending

The other doctrine is our Presbyterian belief that a person continues, by the grace of God, in the Christian life to the end, once faith comes to him. This is because of two things closely related to what has been said concerning election. First, when God bestows his grace on a person it is not simply to save him from sin or even from hell. It is with the express purpose of working in him all through that person's life by his spirit so as finally to have him conform unto the image of his Son. From the very beginning of faith in his life God intends to prepare him for the wonders of eternal life. Had this not been true he would never have poured out his grace upon him at all. Also, the new life which is given with faith is of such a quality that it is called eternal life. We have already seen that the very essence of this new life is love both in relation to our neighbor and to God. This is basically because God's relation to us in redemption is one of love and of such a love that there is nothing that can ever break it down or dissolve it. God will ever love us and continue to give us the quality of life by his Spirit that never ends. Everything that comes to us, then, in this life as Christian, such as our growth in every virtue, is an increasing pledge that ultimately we shall have life that shall be without end. In other words, Election tells us God has loved us from eternity. This view we are now considering, known as "the perseverance of the saints," says he will love us throughout eternity.

(4) The Church Is Linked to Eternity

Up until now our discussion concerning last things has been largely in terms of the individual. It would not be inaccurate to say that what is true of an individual is also applicable to the Church as the body of Christ. Like the individual Christian, the Church is in the world of time and space but it also is essentially a reality belonging to the eternal Kingdom. Its life belongs to the new age which is to come or if we want to think of it in another way the Holy Spirit brings over into this world the values, the graces, and virtues that belong to the Kingdom of God. The Church as a Messianic community upon earth is the vehicle or channel by which concrete expression can be given to realities of an eternal quality. Thus every moment of the historical existence of the Church there come into its life the things that are eternal. The Church itself lives on at its best as a kind of token of that Kingdom of which the prophets dreamed, which Christ firmly established and in which the whole communion of saints will dwell eternally.

2. What Are the Last Things for an Individual?

(1) Death Comes to Every Person

We come now to think about the various elements in the doctrine of last things for each individual. Scripture tells us one's years are three score and ten and then the end comes for him. The writer of Hebrews says every man must die once (Hebrews 9:27). This is because we are finite beings. It is also true that the death of man has always been associated with sin in the Bible. We have seen earlier that sin is what makes death so painful to the mind of a person. Death is the last enemy to strike us on earth and only the Christian may have confidence that death's blow is not the final undoing of him. It is of the very essence of our Christian belief that death is overcome by faith in Christ and He opened up the doors of eternity. The Spirit of God has already given us the quality of life that is triumphant over death (1 Corinthians 2:9, 10). Death does set a limit to our human life and the thoughts of it could be very depressing were it not for the hope of life eternal. This life does in very truth derive its inspiration and significance from the life to come.

(2) The Christian Enters into Fullness of Life at Death

The Shorter Catechism asks the question as to what happens to the Christian at death, and gives a classical answer: "The souls of believers are at their death made perfect in holiness, and do immediately pass into glory; and their bodies, being still united with Christ, do rest in their graves until the resurrection" (Question 37). This answer was written at a time when there was a sharp dualism in thought between the soul and the body. The writers were also concerned to refute the Roman Catholic notion of purgatory. Someone has said they should never have put it like they did because of the difficulty of conceiving our body and soul being separated from each other as is implied in this statement. But this is the only way they could have expressed themselves then. It is true today we think more in terms of the whole personality and we believe both body and soul are necessarily united in the entire person.

3. What Are Heaven and Hell Like?

The following question in the Cathechism asks what benefits Christians receive from Christ at the resurrection. We are told that they shall be raised up in glory, openly acknowledged and acquitted and made perfectly blessed in the full enjoying of God through all eternity (Question 38). Some people find it difficult to think of heaven as a place of perfection and unclouded bliss.

(1) Heaven Is Everlasting Fulfillment

There undoubtedly has been a great deal of unreality about many of the descriptions men have given as to what heaven will be like. We must remember that the Scripture gives us a highly pictorial representation of both the heavenly realities and atmosphere. We may be confident that those who wrote in this fashion in the Bible did not expect a literal usage to be made of their language. We may think of heaven as the attainment of the condition of human existence in which the handicaps, limits, and obstacles that beset us in our earthly life are removed. Our fathers thought of perfection in terms of that which was fixed and unchanging. More recently men and women have found this "static" conception unsatisfying. It may be easier in our thought of this question to approach it in the light of a modern notion of growth not toward perfection, but *within* it. If we regard it in this way we can believe our experience in heaven can grow while at the same time it will be a movement within the realm of perfection.

We have never been able to say that heaven is going to be this or that sort of an existence in a specific manner. Yet in the light of our Christian faith we feel there are some things we can say about it. First, it will be a realm of warm, rich, creative personal relationships with God and all other personal beings. If what we have said about the eternal primacy of love be true, heaven will be the fullest and richest possible expression of this virtue.

Second, we may rest in the confidence that there will be some vital and dynamic form of personal recognition of individuals over there. We are reminded that Scripture often uses the word "see" or "behold him face to face" in a figurative sense and these terms do not mean physical sight. To understand is often spoken of as "seeing." If our existence there is spiritual and if our future bodies are spiritual as Paul intimates, we can well believe that divine power could easily endow them with capacities for personal recognition of a far deeper kind than would be possible through the use of our physical senses.

In the third place, we may think of heaven as an opportunity for fulfillment for our personalities along the line of our highest dreams, deepest urges, and loftiest hopes in this life. The things that we have wanted most to be, the achievements which we have dreamed would be ours, and the growth in our lives at which we have aimed—these and more may be opportunities heaven has in store for all of us.

(2) Hell Is Ultimate Defeat

The thought of hell does not set well with the modern mind. Perhaps there has been too much stress upon a Christianity of fear in some parts of Christendom. Most of us will have a great deal of sympathy with the woman reported to be seen on the streets in a small village of Europe during the Crusades. She was carrying a bucket of water in one hand and a coal of fire in the other. When asked why she was carrying such odd objects she replied, "I am carrying the coal of fire to burn up heaven and the bucket of water to quench the fire of hell so men and women will not serve God for hope of reward or fear of hell." We would all agree that we wish it would not be necessary to have a doctrine about hell. Yet we cannot deny the fact that the Bible has a good bit to say about it. We are reminded of C. S. Lewis' statement on this subject. It is his view that if there isn't a hell God will have a very difficult problem on his hands when the supermen like Hitler and Mussolini get there, if they do not repent. It is possible to conceive they may never repent and may even get worse after death. His question is if there isn't any hell what is God going to do with people like this?

Some of the Church fathers could easily believe in a hell of literal fire and brimstone. Tertullian in the second century and Aquinas in the thirteenth both taught this view of hell. This is even yet the official doctrine of the Roman Catholic Church. A few years ago the picture of the Pope was carried in the American newspapers because he had said that hell is a place of this nature. There has been some variation of opinion about the nature of hell in Protestant thought. John Calvin spoke of the imagery describing hell as pictorial and figurative, and as the inspired effort to describe the awful reality of perdition. This conception in no way diminishes the dreadful fact of what the Bible calls eternal death.

We believe that hell means isolation from God, with vivid memory of the pride, arrogance, and evil that rejected Him. Some have thought that the sins of our life into which we plunged in our rebellion against God will remain a ceaseless torment to conscience. Our pride, vanity, hate, lust, and greed may fill our spirits and frantically haunt us with increased power without opportunity or ability of satisfaction. Perhaps the worst and most awful thing we can say about hell is it is a place of unspeakable loneliness, and of an indescribable sense of utter and endless insecurity.

4. How Shall We Describe the End?

(1) The Return of Christ

The general events connected with last things according to our Presbyterian belief can be described briefly and simply. We do not need charts or maps to set them forth. Our conviction is in God's own good time Christ will return to the earth for judgment. When this is to be no human knows nor can know. It may be soon and it may not be for even thousands of years. When our Lord does return to the earth two main events will take place. There will be the resurrection of the dead and the general judgment. The Bible tells us that those who are alive at the presence of his coming will be caught up with him in the air. We take this to mean that when our Lord does come there will be some who shall not see death. Christian thinkers have usually interpreted the change through which this portion of humanity will pass as that of putting off mortality and putting on immortality. The only experience to which they have ever been able to compare it is that of death. For death is just that—moving away from the mortal into the immortal. Not that it will be death through which they go but it will be as near like death as anything we can imagine.

(2) The Last Judgment

As to the Judgment, we need not think of all the legal scenes, terminology, and associations that are connected with our judicial systems on earth. Judgment means that when God finally makes his great disclosure in Christ, every man will be confronted by holy, divine presence and that every one of us shall be called upon to give an account of his life to his Creator. It has been said the best illustration we have of what the Judgment will be like is that scene at the trial of our Lord when he penetratingly looked into the eyes of the guilty apostle Peter. We are told that Peter went out and wept bitterly. As the glance of our Lord then was enough to convict him of his guilt, the presence of God in Christ at the end will be judgment enough.

As the early Christians believed, the Judgment for those of faith is not something to be feared or looked forward to with fear and anxiety. It is the moment in which truth will be declared more powerful than error, light to be desired more than darkness, good will be triumphant, and evil will be destroyed. Those who are "openly acknowledged and acquitted" through the redemptive work of Christ will then enter that eternal realm to live forever with the God of glory and his people. Then we shall know fully even as also we shall be fully known. What shall we know? What life means? What God is like? What love is? In knowing this we shall know it all.

The story is told of an old woman and a young lad, about twelve years of age, riding together in the Metro in Paris. (This is what we call the subway.) The car was jogging along at a rapid speed and swaying noticeably as it rushed on under the earth. Suddenly it lurched and the passengers were shaken about. Just then the old woman put out her hand and tried to steady the boy—one would guess he was her grandson—he looked at her in anger and his entire body stiffened as if to say, "Let me alone, I can quite take care of myself." She met his defiant look with a warm, gracious smile. When he saw it, his face also lighted up in joyous response and they stood there looking at each other as if there was perfect understanding between them. Then the person who relates this scene remarks: In this fragment of time and experience, in this exchange of smiles between these two persons there is revealed all there is to know on earth and in heaven. What else is there to know but love in the presence of God?

Suggested Reading:

> *Call to Faith*, Chapter 10.
> *Confession of Faith*, Chapters 34, 35.
> Scripture, Matthew 24, 25; Mark 13; 1 Corinthians 15:1–28; 1 Thessalonians 5; Revelation 21, 22.